Forever Home Within
~ An Ivory Castle

By

Vanessa Bunting
www.foreverhomewithin.com

Shield Crest

ISBN: 978-1-912505-82-1

A CIP catalogue record for this book
is available from the British Library

MMXX

Published by
ShieldCrest Publishing Ltd
86 Springhill Road
Aylesbury, Buckinghamshire, HP18 0TF
England.
www.shieldcrest.co.uk
Tel: +44 (0)333 8000 890

To you dear reader wherever you are...

 ...in a car, on a plane, boat or train, on holiday, in a waiting room,
church, library or hospital - sharing spaces and time with others,
   or if you're now on your own at home, these words might be of some interest and amusement to you, for a while.

This is my intention at least but if you should become bored at any stage, please don't force yourself to read on, just go and get another book!

Cheers!

Vanessa

The mountain goat looks up not down
It rarely turns around
It sometimes stays and rests a while
Its feet on solid ground

The climb may seem quite daunting
A strain on every limb
But the mountain goat looks on not back
It has the will to win

It knows the path is rocky
and others may decline
But one more step – and there it is
The top of the world is mine!

R. C. Barlow

FOREWORD

Yes, I'm still here, still searching, still hoping, still dreaming and still believing that my forever home awaits… somewhere.

In the meantime, life goes on, times change, and perceptions change which enables me to continue writing about my particular experiences and thoughts about them.

If there isn't enough already to take in to account, such as health, finances, relationships, employment, safety and so on, there's still the need to think about what's right by us as individuals and whether we're fulfilling our soul's desire. For me, I yearn for a permanent dwelling place with a decent standard of lifestyle whilst enjoying harmonious relationships. I've already found a desirable area to settle but it's hundreds of miles away and so not near enough to visit as much as I'd like.

However, I remain convinced by the instinctive search of a better life, i.e. what *feels* right, rather than the conventional checklist relating to: property price, desirable location, good return on investment and so on.

Whilst not looking to live in an ivory coloured castle as such, a forever home to me would be any property that feels like a familiar home where I feel safe, secure and nurtured for the rest of my life, with my husband and cats and maybe dogs.

I think it's vital to follow your heart – whilst also listening to your head and partner of course – and although it's tempting to move nearer to family and friends, I cannot ignore the special place I've found which has captured my heart and imagination. All I need to do now, is find *that* property.

Moving somewhere relatively unknown is a risky step, especially when there's not even the guarantee of an adequate income to live on, but I believe this is one risk worth taking.

I've only to be mindful of the elusive eel (those slippery snake-like creatures which live in some of our lakes, rivers and even moats) to know why I trust my gut feeling. The life-cycle of the eel is very intriguing and starts with larvae hatching in the Sargasso Sea (North Atlantic) and being carried on the current of the Gulf Stream for a few years and a few thousand miles, by which time they have grown into elvers (small eels) and reach Britain (amongst other countries) to slither their way across land towards their ancestral home. How do they know where that place is when they haven't been there before? Once there, they'll live in the lake, river, moat or wherever, for seven to nineteen years before slithering their way back to a river which leads to the sea, to make the same journey back to the Sargasso Sea where they will spawn and die—and their larvae begins the same epic journey all over again. This is what they know they have to do, and so they do it—

despite all the risks involved. If ever there was a tale of livelihood being directed by instinct, this has to be a fine example.

By comparison, my decision to head for the hills (literally) in the belief that everything will turn out for the best, seems to be a pretty safe bet to me. So, whatever happens next towards reaching this idyll, will be documented right here with the same openness and honest way I know.

Every castle has a story to tell.

Here is mine.

Vanessa

CONTENTS

Chapters:

Illustrations:

Chapter 1

Let Battle Commence!

After all the festivities surrounding Christmas and the new year, I looked around the bare lounge and the now empty corner where the artificial Christmas tree had stood. It was now carefully packed away in the loft, together with all the fairy lights and adornments. I wondered where our tree would be sited the following year–in another lounge, in another home, in another county?

It was the start of 2019 and the house was getting back to normal—being clean, tidy and aired. The cats, Issy, Clipsey, Whingey, Foz and Alice had just been fed and we (my husband Tony and I) were enjoying a cup of tea whilst relaxing at home. That's not to say that this is a once-a-year occurrence, but it was a welcome moment before my thoughts turned to Tony's return to work in a few days' time.

Tony looked across at the little pile of extra special Christmas cards I'd put to one side. He knew I'd be packing them away in a lockable decorative trunk, where I put all my keepsakes and special letters. He asked: "You'd better tell me where the key is to that trunk because, if you pop your clogs, I'll need to get everything out of there and burn it!"

I laughed just like I always do at his semi-playful take on my unusual ways and my laughing seemed to encourage him further: "Scrap the key then," he said, "I'll take the whole trunk of junk and burn the lot!"

I laughed again and louder this time. Our ideas about being organised clearly differed but in any case; what's to say *I'll* be 'popping my clogs' first?!

Of all the people in the world to choose from, Tony and I spend the most time we have with each other—even though we are quite different characters. I've had a few long-term relationships in my life; and one ended up like a brother and sister kinship because we had so much in common and were, too much, like peas from the same pod. Now with Tony, I think it's more a case of opposites being attracted to each other, even though we still share similar values and ideals. There are those times when we disagree, and our relationship becomes confrontational and warlike. Thankfully, those times are not often. We both have a sense of protection towards each other, our cats, our home and our lifestyle which is bound by a silent pledge of something powerful and intangible; I take this to be love.

Nevertheless, if there's one thing I've learned from past years, it's the importance of having some sort of structure and strategy in my life in order to feel organised, focussed and ready for whatever happens next. So, having literally got my house in order (in my way), packed my cards away and bagged up all my unwanted clothes ready for the charity shop, I felt duly ready to face the year ahead.

As with many people, I was looking forward to a fresh start after a not-so-brilliant previous year and somehow New Year is a good place to start even though it's just another day. But this time I wanted to be more proactive about making things happen rather than just be on the receiving end of whatever life brings my way—which is what usually happens (and where family illness is concerned, it cannot be any other way of course).

As I sipped my tea, I reminded myself of how fortunate I was because I have every basic need in life which matters to me personally. They are (in no particular order):

- Fresh air
- Adequate sleep
- Warmth and security
- Cleanliness (home and self)
- Enough food to eat
- Enough water to drink
- Companionship and friendship (just a few) – be it human, feline, flora or fauna
- Peace of mind (most of the time)

I thought I had everything covered and whilst keeping the list to myself, I asked Tony what *he* regarded as the most important things in life. He thought for a while, and said:

- To be healthy
- Financially secure with a very nice house and car
- Happy and content with yours truly and the cats

I dare say that Tony's listing is more lavish than mine and on a higher level of ideals compared to my basic and instinctive needs which I place above everything else. It's not that I don't have aspirations, because I do, but I'm very mindful of not taking the basics for granted because, without them, we cannot actually function at all!

Throughout January, whilst Tony was out at work, I carried on with my quest to blitz the house of any dust and dirt by cleaning, polishing and bleaching almost everything in sight (and out of sight). I went at it with more gusto than usual because I wanted to counteract the recent overindulgences in all things calorific and so I used this opportunity to use as much energy as possible. It probably made little difference, but I felt better for trying—and the house benefitted too.

The next morning, the phone rang – it was the estate agent to ask if a couple could view our house the very next day – oh and by the way, they're cash buyers. Well, knock me down with a feather! Our house had been up for sale for a few months and so this was fabulous news. I was so glad that they didn't want to arrive immediately because I wanted time to look my best. Yes, tomorrow would be perfectly fine, and both the house and I myself would be looking as good as we possibly could (Tony would be out at work).

I called Tony and told him the news. He sounded excited as he mentioned that, should an offer be made on our house, we would have to go and view our online 'saved' properties straight away. It was all starting to get exciting but until someone actually made an offer on our home, it would remain unsold. So far, we'd had no viewings at all, but then it was a quiet time, the winter months.

The following day was beautifully sunny and so was perfect for highlighting all the positives about the house such as the airy and light lounge, the cheerful and spacious garden and a very pleasing outlook across acres of farmland.

The appointment for the viewing had been made for 1.30 p.m. but at 1.45 there was still no sign of anyone. I started to worry. The phone rang and I sort of knew that the viewing was cancelled—and the estate agent's apologetic tone confirmed as much, as he went on to say that Mr & Mrs Cash-Buyer had just found another home to buy. So that was that then: Twenty-four hours of high hopes followed by about twenty-four minutes of dashed dreams, and I wasn't going to dwell on the disappointment a second longer. I was just thankful that I hadn't told anyone else about the booked viewing, so it saved me explaining the non-viewing to everyone else. Tony was naturally disappointed too but, like me, he didn't regard it as the end of the world. It showed that buyers were starting to come out and look, so maybe the following week or month we'd be lucky.

It was back to routine again, but I did have a couple of creative flourishes to brighten up our life. Firstly, I decided to upgrade the hallway a little. We couldn't afford to decorate or buy new flooring but the small cupboard door under the stairs did need a revamp—especially as the hallway is the first impression one has when one enters the house. I initially thought about painting the door, but the single block of colour might not be an improvement, so how about feature wallpaper? I looked online and found wallpaper which looked like book shelves. I ordered it straight away, along with a paste brush and paste. All I had to do was wait for it to arrive and then get going on the transformation.

Tony wasn't as enthusiastic or as visionary about the door but reserved judgement until it was done.

Within the next week, we both worked together and agreed that the hallway was now more welcoming without being out of character of the house. I know it's personal taste and someone else might change the door or hallway layout itself, but whilst we were still there I didn't see why we couldn't continue loving the house with small enhancements which may help with an eventual trade-off. Some battles can indeed be fought with good intentions and I, for one, prefer it this way.

On the subject of personal taste, I decided it was time to upgrade my Victoria Sponge cake. I have made various cakes over the years but, by far, enjoy making and eating the Victoria Sponge the most—with freshly whipped cream in the centre. Usually it's made with raspberry jam and maybe some local fruit like blackcurrants or blackberries from the garden but now I had an urge to create a citrus version. So, this time I used lemon curd on each side of the sponge and then topped the cream with mandarin slices (from a tin and strained). It looked and tasted delicious and I knew I could add this to my Victoria Sponge repertoire. The next version was going to be a chocolate sponge made with real melted chocolate and cherry jam on the cake with glacé cherries on the cream—a sort of Black Forest Gateaux Victoria Sponge. It goes to show that you *can* be a successful one-trick pony!

Just quickly, this is my citrus Victoria Sponge cake with lemon curd and mandarin recipe—really easy to make; just 4 oz self-raising flour (sifted), 4 oz caster sugar, 4 oz total margarine & butter (whatever you have more of is the greater weight), 2 eggs, a few splashes of vanilla essence and a pinch of salt (I use rock salt). Combine all in a food mixer and put into a greased cake tin and 180 degrees preheated oven (fan oven in my case) for 20 mins or until the top is bouncy. Then just empty on to a cooling rack before transferring to a large plastic lid or chopping board (the cake should still be upside down). Using a pallet knife, spread the lemon curd over the whole cake then cut in half and slightly separate. Then whip double cream (small pot) until thick and spread on the top of one half. Strain the tinned mandarins from the tin and carefully place on the cream before topping with the other half of the cake. Sprinkle with icing sugar from the sieve and voila! Essentially, it's half of a perfect cake which does last for up to three days in the fridge (a large, whole cake would end up being thrown away) so it's a fabulously delicious afternoon treat with a nice cup of tea.

At this time, in my daily life, I also heard some

uplifting news stories. The first was about the plight of stray dogs in Italy during the cold winter nights when they had nowhere else to go. Well, the staff of a well-known furniture store there opened the doors to allow stray dogs to sleep in the store during the night – and so they did (although obviously not draped all over the furnishings). Some staff and customers ended up adopting some of the dogs and others provided food. How lovely and kind of all involved and just reading about it made me feel wonderful.

Another story was about a little pet rabbit who lived in a farmhouse in Wales. Every morning he'd be let outside where he'd run towards a flock of sheep and spend the day with them frolicking around with the lambs—it actually showed video footage which was lovely. Then near the end of the day, the rabbit would return home for his feed and sleep until the morning, when his amazing life would start all over again.

Finally, a guy was walking his whippet dog along an everyday street in the UK. He passed a green telephone junction box and as he did so, he noticed something moving around behind it: it was a magpie which had been injured so he picked it up and took it home to care for it, which he and his partner did admirably. Now the magpie lives with them and feeds with the dog, goes for walks with them and even drinks beer in the pub! The magpie is quite a character and a real chatterbox who's as happy as he can be.

I expect these stories and videos can be found on the internet quite easily if you wanted to know the full story.

On a lesser scale of positivity, we had our own unusual scenario to deal with ….

One morning, I saw our neighbour's cat (Percy) in our lounge. It wasn't so unusual for Percy to come through the cat flap and eat whatever cat food was still available and so I didn't take much notice of him. However, as the day wore on, Percy hadn't moved from his curled-up position on the mat and his black-and-white coat was barely moving from his breathing. I started to worry that Percy was ill and so I put some food down next to him. He ignored the food but did move, taking refuge behind the sofa. Clearly, he wanted to be left alone.

Thankfully, I was able to contact the neighbours, to whom Percy belonged, and I told them about the situation. They came straight round to our house to collect Percy and said that his plight had been caused by two main factors: firstly, Percy had stayed outside since Christmas because the neighbour's grandchildren had been over to stay and were too noisy for his liking—this is quite a regular occurrence apparently. Secondly, just recently, Percy had his booster vaccination which comprised a single cocktail of vaccines in one jab which had, ironically, affected his wellbeing. (This is true of a couple of our cats too, as they appear to be under the weather for a few days after their vaccinations.)

So, after 12-year-old poorly Percy had been hauled out from behind our sofa, his 'mum' told us that her grandchildren were gone now, so Percy could go back to sleeping on his special bed in front of the radiator in the warmth. If he didn't improve, they'd be taking him back to the vet. Percy did fully recover within a few weeks and is now back to his usual self in the neighbourhood.

It was now the start of Tony's four days off work and as the weather was still very cold, our initial attention was on some pipework outside the back door which was leaking through a crack. This is one of those incredibly boring problems, in my opinion and yet we have to devote time, effort and money in order to 'stop it getting worse'. Luckily, Tony is very adept in this respect, but we still ended up driving to various stores in order to find the specific pipework, brackets and lagging required. Then Tony spent the whole of the following day sorting out this quite urgent task because if the water had frozen in the pipe, then the backed-up water could end up in the house. The problem was solved for the foreseeable future and so another battle was fought and won.

Our recent conversations with friends and family were of a similar vein in terms of needing to react to whatever life brings: some friends had travelled to visit their friends in Europe and having emerged from the specific airport, they'd been greeted by their friends who they'd hugged and greeted only to find, moments later, that both their passports had been stolen! There was nothing that could be done but to apply for new passports and then wait for them to arrive at their friends' place before they could fly home again. It was fortunate that they would be staying for a number of weeks and so there was time enough to get organised before returning. Nevertheless, it was very upsetting for all concerned. The replacement passports arrived in France separately and one arrived on the day of departure back to the UK so by the time our friends had raced to the airport, they only had ten minutes to spare! It was all very hairy, but they managed to get back to the UK on their scheduled flight—and oh how glad they were to be back. I said I'd make them one of my citrus cakes when they next visited us.

Another friend who'd had numerous visits to the dentist to sort out a tooth extraction – which you'd think by its nature would be a once only visit – then had the distress of dealing with her poorly husband who had a strange rash on each leg and so was prescribed various creams and lotions by the doctor. His recovery was extremely slow and, still dealing with her tooth problem, she then found that their son (who lives at home with them) had contracted shingles and so he was laid up and poorly too! They are all okay now, but it was a weekly saga as to how life was going for them.

The final piece of disappointing news came from a relative who'd been having trouble at work and was feeling undermined and undervalued by some staff members who'd seemed intent of making things unnecessarily difficult. I was asked for some advice about whether to whistle-blow or resign and then look for another job. I wasn't sure that coming to me for advice in this respect was necessarily the right thing to do because I have no more answers than anyone else but I can give my opinion which is to say: it's unfortunate that bad behaviour in the workplace still happens today and no matter who you are or where you stand in the company, there will always be people who rile you every now and then. It's a human condition—people will always be people and so what they think and what they do is not for us to question. However, when their actions create discomfort and ill will, then we can look at our own options. Obviously if there is a misconduct issue involved, then I'd definitely refer the matter to senior management. But for everyday interactions which basically become a battle of wills for the most part, then I would consider removing myself from this unjust culture as quickly as possible. It's as simple as that, in my opinion; I know it's not easy if you're reliant upon the salary but I know from personal experience that if you end up being in the wrong place at the wrong time and maybe for the wrong reasons, it will eat away at you and potentially affect your health through lack of sleep. In this instance, within days, she'd handed in her notice and found another job almost straight away and hasn't looked back for a second.

Life is too short to suffer unnecessarily and there are always alternatives to any choices we make, regardless of how far down the line we've come. I would always advocate asking *yourself* how you feel and what you'd like to do for your sake and no-one else's. This is not about being selfish, it's about being self-respectful. By the same token, I would not suggest taking any action to spite someone else such as   refusing an alternative job at work because it would suit the perpetrator and let them off the hook. There are never any winners where spite is involved and there's even less chance of anyone flourishing and prospering under such a negative regime.

Before February was out, Tony and I developed flu-like symptoms with fever and weakness to the point where Tony had to take time off work. For me, the daily routine of making drinks, small amounts of food and tidying and cleaning was about all I could do. The beautiful sunny weather outside was wasted on us and whilst we attempted a walk in the fresh air, we ended up sitting on a bench not far from home and comparing notes about who'd had the least sleep and who felt the most drained! How we ever went for long walks and cycle rides appeared to be a mystery at that point as we came to terms with our temporary suspension from living our lives. Recovery was slow and given that both of us were off our food, I had to be mindful of Tony's diabetes and ensure that we still ate regularly. The strangest thing is, I'd been off wine for weeks, which has happened before for no apparent reason and so I just avoided it. Now with the reduced food intake, I became aware of the new need to reduce both because we simply didn't need as much food and alcohol as we used to. This is an age thing I think and obviously our illness meant that even less food was required. I started to use much smaller serving bowls which were more than adequate for our needs and even though Tony had seen a doctor during this time, it was still a waiting game whilst keeping warm and drinking plenty which was to be our salvation from this nasty virus. Three weeks later, we were just about getting back on track and looking forward to being fighting fit again.

However, during this time, we had amused ourselves with music, television, computer games, reading, and generally daydreaming in my case.

February is the month where I'm reminded of a special couple from the past: Vicki and Cyril, who lived at the flats in London where Mum and I had lived very happily in the late 1970s. Vicki and Cyril were no longer with us but Cyril's birthday was in February and his dear wife Vicki passed away one February, two days before his birthday, it was so terribly sad. Cyril was heartbroken and struggled to live without Vicki. He died two years later. Sometimes I look at my own life with Tony and the cats which is similar to the life Vicki and Cyril had with their cats—no children or social circle, just themselves all together as one unit and appreciating all that they had. They too had been on the move from home to home in search of their elusive *forever home* which they never found but yet were grounded within themselves and content with their lot amidst the community spirit which existed as many of us became acquainted.

About thirty years ago, Vicki gave me a drinks coaster with a picture of a grey tabby cat sitting in a garden. The cat looked like my cat Winston and now our tabby cat Foz. I use the coaster every day as it's on my bedside cabinet and the picture is still as vibrant with the laminate intact. I also use Cyril's cotton neck scarves as make-up cloths and so this couple remains as a part of my life today and always, wherever I live.

Another couple who I'm reminded of who also lived at the flats at that time, were friends Eileen and Esme who moved from Rhodesia (now Zimbabwe). They were a very interesting and humorous couple who often joined our little group in the communal gardens, on a sunny day, for a natter over tea and cake. Eileen and Esme's flat was impeccably kept and furnished with many African artefacts including two hand-carved pictures of village life, which they told me were made from the Mukwa tree. I'd admired the pictures but didn't expect to receive them as a gift for my new home when I left for Essex in 1981. I still have those pictures on my wall today and feel proud to be a custodian of them as I remember those two very special people.

The final 'significant person' from those memorable days in London, is my dear friend Abigail with whom I have kept in touch, ever since. There may not have been the London cafe culture with all the squashy sofas, artisan coffee, broadsheet newspapers and buzz of activity found today, but there was a place in our little garden where a meeting of minds and souls not only stood the test of time, but endures to this day; even with those who have passed on.

When I think back to those days, I realise that my life changed completely when I moved to Essex. I had been blissfully happy living with Mum at our flat whilst not only enjoying the company of our friendly neighbours but having those scenic walks through the local park, taking trips to the shops and visiting family and friends. Mum and I were good friends, yet our relationship was very much an old-fashioned mother and daughter pecking order which suited me as I was still a teenager at the time. If I hadn't moved to Essex, I dare say that life would have changed anyway because Mum met her second husband and they moved away to Norfolk so it would have been unlikely that I would have afforded to live in the flat by myself. I may have stayed in London, but life would still have been different without Mum.

My initial experience of living in Essex was very good: I was welcomed in the office at work, along with a few other 'relocatees from London' and met lots of interesting people. My job was basically the same so no real changes there. The flat where I initially lived was perfectly suitable, until I was burgled. I moved to another property and was very happy for a number of years until some drug-users moved in next door which resulted on my receiving an accidental needle-stick injury from one of their rubbish bags outside my house. And so, I moved house again to the cottage where I thought 'this is it'. Whilst still in Essex, my employers then asked me to return to work in London, which I did but I found that my allocated job was more complex and coupled with the travel each day with train disruptions and cancellations, I started to struggle. I was also waiting for the test results from my blood samples from *that* needle-stick injury which took six months in those days—the result was clear, but I felt far from euphoric. On reflection, it was probably no wonder that I had an emotional meltdown and felt that I'd literally come to the end of the road. To cap it all, my faithful dog, Gypsy, had to be put to sleep due to cancer and then a few months later, my dad died from cancer too.

For me and my constantly frightened existence, life was suddenly a waiting game until those shredded nerves repaired themselves and a sense of calmness returned which allowed my mind to take charge once more. I tried to reason why it had happened and then how it had happened (scientifically) to make sense of a very bewildering time of my life. I concluded that we are more than a mass of physical and mental, we are also emotional and spiritual—all of which needs equal care and consideration, however deep within ourselves they may be.

Throughout my personal ordeal, there remained a small flicker of hope that I would get through it, and this gave me the courage to find a way towards carving out a new life. I knew there'd be changes and life would never be the same as before, because I was now a different person: I was someone who knew, first hand, about the fragility of being human. This is why I wrote a book called *Forever Home Within* because it doesn't matter where you live or who you are because external factors will always impact on your life and therefore play a part in your response and decision-making.

Ultimately, what matters most, is how you feel inside and if you feel like I did, when I thought that I'd just carry on regardless no matter what life throws at me, then I'd urge you to think again because too much of 'carrying on regardless', suggests that life is about appeasing others and not necessarily feeding your own soul—your birthright to happiness. We are not machines or superheroes, but our egos might have it that way if we choose to ignore who we *really* are.

I was never cut out for a career in the City and yet stayed with the same company for twenty years. But I have no regrets because the job allowed me a certain amount of financial security and independence—and now I'm here conveying my thoughts about the importance of understanding one's self and inner fulfilment. Do not allow anyone to suggest that their agenda is more important than yours. Obviously, the exception is the workplace where employers can dictate the job role and pay, but then you can spend the money on whatever *you* like! I know this is basic stuff but I'm just saying let's not forget that we are all individual spirits with differing needs so make sure those needs are met at some stage—keeping that inner spirit alive, well and listened to.

Tony does not share my sentiment about life in London (which he experienced too in the past) – which is fine of course – but I do feel very nostalgic when I think back to those days. I always will. There's no disputing that I am a country girl at heart who loves animals, unspoilt countryside and all things woodland—but a part of me belongs to London, the City and the amazing people I lived amongst and worked with, at that time.

Fast forward forty years and as we approach March 2019, my thoughts turn once again to the renewal of my patent for the bottle stand idea (apologies to those I've already bored with this!). It was an idea I had to create a holder for bottles in the updise down position to allow all the contents to drain at one end and so reduce waste by early disposal. Maybe this is one battle in which I should admit defeat and walk away from—but not just yet. The last email message I'd received from the interested UK company was a number of months ago to say that they'd be contacting me in the spring once they'd decided whether to add it to their new collection of household items. Although I'm tempted to send an email reminder, there's Brexit still to happen (or not as the case may be) and I dare say that a confirmation wouldn't be forthcoming at this point. So, I will wait a little longer and then send a reminder if necessary. I think that deep down, I just don't want the answer to be a 'no' and so while I'm waiting for an answer, there's the constant 'maybe' hanging in the air. I can live with 'maybe'. There was a time, not so long ago, when I would have insisted on a decisive answer straight away and if I didn't like the answer, I'd quickly move on and keep asking the same question until I had the answer I wanted. Patience may be a virtue, but it can also encourage procrastination.

At this time and in many aspects of life it seems, there are many 'maybes' hanging around and here's another one: Maybe I should have called this book 'Almost But Not Quite' because this could then apply to the job I never quite nailed down after leaving the insurance industry, or establishing the bottle stand or creating a business like a bed and breakfast, or indeed finding that Forever Home but then what sort of read would a book like that provide? Probably something like 'oh well, I tried this and then gave up, I tried that and then gave up, I threw in the towel on that prospect, and I've given up even contemplating the likelihood of any dreams coming true ever!'

Surely, it's far better to keep fighting for what you want – even if it's in thought only – than to give up on your dreams entirely? Our dreams are the most unique and important part of who we are as individuals – as the stars that we are - and however much they may become trampled upon by life's daily events and inconveniences, they should always remain a lighted beacon within ourselves to help direct us towards a destination which is right for us.

If this seems a bit too cheesy and unrealistic, then I'll put it another way: all the while you're taking time to be offended about what someone else has said or done, or bemoaning how life is always an uphill struggle, then you're not setting time aside to daydream and think about ways to realise your dreams. Furthermore, as soon as you start putting your hopes for the future into the spotlight as being really important, I think you'll feel a lot better about life in general. I speak from vast experience and innumerable mistakes! Now I just keep fighting whether literally or internally because I have no regrets just determination to succeed and ultimately 'Seize the Day' or 'Carpe Diem' as they say!

Chapter 2

Rolling With It

It was the beginning of March and I felt that it was time for some action on the house front. After weeks of there being no viewings on our house, I thought it might be a good idea to focus on the houses on our wish list instead. We could still go and view those properties and have a much-needed enjoyable weekend away at the same time. As we already knew, seeing perfectly suitable houses online was never going to replace the actual experience of being there and knowing for sure.

I put my suggestion to Tony who was certainly interested and with his usual pragmatic approach, took pen to paper and calculated once again how much we could possibly afford, in conjunction with an estimated price for our house and overall moving costs. It was all doable but we would need more than four properties to view (in the Welsh Borders) to make it worth our while; after all, the last time we booked viewings there, one of the properties had sold just before we'd arrived!

So, with this new impetus to carry on regardless, I felt invigorated about good times ahead although we would need to wait a few weeks in order to fully recover from flu. Only then could we arrange the hotel booking and cat care. For now, though, we decided to go for a walk in the sunshine and talk some more about when we could go and whether our neighbours would feed our cats again. Whenever we talked about our plans together, we seemed to connect in a way that diminished all other aspects of life—which wasn't hard to do at the moment as dull routines tended to dominate.

I don't know if it was our new-found energy or subconscious premonition involved, but just before we left for our walk, the phone rang. It was the estate agent to say that a couple would like to view our house that day, in the afternoon! Well, what fabulous news and so instead of going for that walk (and carrying on regardless as we'd intended) we set about getting the house looking as presentable as possible. Tony was out in the garden mowing the lawn to resemble a bowling green whilst I was running around the house and removing various cushions, cat blankets, cat food bowls, foot stalls and any other cluttery paraphernalia I could lay my hands on, then stashing them away in various cupboards and drawers until after the viewing. I even resorted to the finishing touch of polishing the bathroom taps. I then changed into presentable clothing and applied more make-up. Tony did the same—except for the make-up! And we had about half an hour to spare before the first and maybe the *only* viewing necessary.

So in walked the couple booked to view our house. They were very boisterous with big personalities and asking to see the garden first. Of course, it was a pleasure to show them around and they were interested in the trees at the bottom of garden – asking if they had preservation orders on them – which they didn't. I then heard the husband saying to Tony that he has two large garages and a lock-up full of motorbikes and stuff which he had to sort out. I wondered why they were looking at our house with its one garage and no outbuildings— unless they were thinking about cutting the trees down and placing a large outbuilding there? Anyway, the viewing went well, and they looked at the garage before leaving.

Afterwards I'd said to Tony that I didn't think they'd be making an offer to buy our house—it was just a feeling I had. Two days later the agent called and said that the couple had liked the house but wanted something more rural (yes, maybe with those necessary outbuildings!).

So that was that. Gone was the jolly up-tempo approach to grabbing life with both hands and in its place came the 'what's the point of doing anything' mode of thinking. I found these thoughts hard to shift and although Tony didn't *appear* to be bothered one way or another, I knew he was bothered because he said that in future, we shouldn't go to any trouble whatsoever when viewings were booked, but just carry on with our plans. He then went very quiet for the following week and neither of us spoke about a trip away or doing anything else actually. It was quite bizarre that we should feel so down but there we are—the prospect of starting a new life in the country was on par with the current countdown to Brexit—being highly speculative, irritatingly frustrating and not necessarily destined to succeed, in my opinion!

I totally understood why Tony suggested we shouldn't try so hard to get the house ready for viewings in future (although I will never allow the house to look messy).

It's strange how external factors can directly impact on our attitudes and energy levels but then our behaviour can directly impact on our lifestyle and the choices we make too. Keeping a balanced view and everything in perspective was very important right then if we were to continue with our plans.

Quite fittingly, the weather turned very cold and extremely windy from storm Gareth. This lasted for several days. I mostly did stuff around the house but as soon as Tony had a day off work, I suggested we drive out to somewhere locally and maybe have a walk - which we did – but it wasn't for long because the gale-force winds made it almost impossible to talk! Back in the car, we agreed that hosting a Bed & Breakfast business in an area popular with ramblers was far preferable to us than belonging to such groups and their hikes! We were showing signs of ageing and preferred our tried and tested comforts these days.

Towards the end of March, the sun returned again and with the increase of daylight hours, our garden was brimming with budding shrubs and trees just ready to burst into bloom. The birds were chirping loudly, and the occasional bee could be seen slowly bobbing around. Our moods had lifted considerably and so we decided to have another day out and maybe incorporate a pub lunch where we could talk about another trip away to the west country which was still on our minds.

Well, our day out was mostly enjoyable – the sun had shone, we'd enjoyed a walk around a village, had a pub lunch and on our way home, chose a detour which meant us stopping at another pretty Essex village. But this time, the car park which was usually empty but for a few cars, was now completely full but for one space which we managed to squeeze in to despite the double-parked vehicles all around us. Why it was so busy I didn't know because the village was quiet (it was a Monday) but most of the shops were either closed down or changed (back) into residential dwellings (which might explain the full car park). I felt sad for the place because it's previous charm had been somewhat lost to progress and modernisation. My last visit had been about four years back so changes had taken place very quickly. As a traditionalist, I feel sad when changes are so severe, that the original appearance of a property or street is no longer visible.

Not to be put off, we headed towards a large shop which we loved and was just a few miles further on—it sold many delicacies including artisan cakes and pastries and so we thought we'd stop by and pick something up for teatime. However, upon our approach to the shop, we noticed some large concrete blocks strategically placed across the entrance to the car park so we couldn't park; then we saw the large dark empty building behind it—the whole shop had closed down for good. This was another surprise as, again, it was probably only a few years ago since our last visit and it was always such a busy store (we found out later that the shop had to close, reluctantly, after many years of trading. There wasn't a reason given).We drove home and even then, noticed our route was littered with excessive pieces of rubbish strewn across the central reservation of the carriageway and had most likely got there by being thrown from moving vehicles.

I'm not about to dismiss Essex as being a lost cause because it isn't and in fact there are still so many beautiful areas within it. But in that single day, I hadn't seen or experienced the usual day out I'd come to expect from living there. It proved to both Tony and I that our ongoing search for properties and places reminiscent of times past, was not so surprising after all.

I wasted no time in booking our trip away for a few days, having confirmed the dates with our neighbours who'd kindly agreed to feed our cats as before, and I booked the first viewing to one of our 'saved' properties. My rationale was that we might as well act as though we were intending to move house even though in real terms we could not physically make it happen. Somehow this rationale sort of made sense to me - a sort of 'proof' to the Universe that we were serious about moving. Also, the dates I chose to go away were specific by being exactly the same number of days from the beginning of January, as the number of days before the end of last year, when we last went, and so an exact reflection. This also happened to be the only time our neighbours were free to feed our cats for the next month, so I hoped it paid off!

Until then and getting back to reality, I popped into a local supermarket and was confronted by a large display of hot cross buns which looked absolutely delicious. Yes, Easter would soon be here and so most supermarkets would have their shelves stacked with chocolate eggs and other goodies at this time of year – some things never change – or do they? I was really looking forward to my tea time with Tony and our toasted, buttered buns but when I opened the packaging, there was a strange smell and not at all spicy as I'd expected. They looked very much like the real deal with the cross on the top and had a lovely squidgy texture but when I checked the label, it pronounced 'Salted Caramel and Chocolate Chip Buns'. Excuse my ignorance but what's going on here - and where are my hot cross buns?! I dared to try a piece, as did Tony and we both pulled a funny face at each other – oh well, the birds can have them instead, we decided. I do like chocolate and salted caramel as a dessert in its own right and so I felt both annoyed and duped (even though it was my fault for not checking the label – I should have learned lessons about label changing since my last encounter with basmati rice becoming 'pure' basmati rice).

Without further ado, I pulled my favourite cook book from the kitchen drawer (the one I received 'free' with my first cooker I'd purchased in 1981 (and it worked perfectly well for 25 years). I looked up 'hot cross buns' whilst muttering to myself, "How hard can they be to make?" Amazingly, I had all the necessary ingredients to hand and so I set about making my very first batch of hot cross buns and about two hours later: voila! the real deal, although I chose not to put a buttery cross on the top or a sugar glaze (even though it was a bit late for calorie counting). Even more amazingly, the buns were delicious and authentic—and the house smelt of proper hot cross buns. But of course, the real test is having adequate approval from my nearest and dearest. Tony said nothing as he munched his way through but afterwards declared that they were better than the shop buns and I should make them every single weekend! Yay! I won't be making buns every weekend of course but this was a classic case of turning a disappointment in to a very pleasant surprise and, to be honest, I wouldn't have taken on the challenge without that inner annoyance which had powered my determination.

At that time, some international news came through which paled my worrying about the flavour of buns into total insignificance: A terrible cyclone, 'Idai', had struck Southern Africa: Mozambique, Zimbabwe and other surrounding countries. The devastation was clear to see on the TV screen with bridges now gone and raging torrents of brown water rushing by. Hundreds had died, apparently. It was distressing to see the filming of people trapped in trees where they'd been for days, but thankfully reassuring to see those people being winched to safety via a helicopter rescue. Some villages were cut off from each other by the flooding which made any rescue attempts even more difficult.

Some days later, the following news on the disaster mentioned the growing threat of famine, diseases and illnesses which the hospitals couldn't cope with. After then seeing the film footage of people weak and seriously ill in hospital, there came the inevitable appeal for help with every aspect of loss which these disasters tend to create. Tony and I were both saddened by this news, but we weren't surprised about the appeals launched, because we'd seen the same sorry state of affairs involving famine and disease for decades—and they're still happening. Why is that? In this day and age of modern technology and obtainable resources, there surely could be measures put in place to alleviate the effects of such disasters. Is it Mother Nature dishing out more water these days to facilitate the ever-increasing human population or is it really manmade by the global warming we're all contributing to, in our everyday consumerism of all things heat and hot water orientated?

Just when I started to feel very serious about life and our planet at this time, some further UK news came through, relaying that a scientist has calculated that we may run out of drinking water in the next twenty-five years! Did I hear right, I wondered? How much more rain do we have to have, to avoid this outcome?! There were plenty of flood warnings in the UK these days. But, if drought really was a possibility, then let's get building some more reservoirs immediately and whilst we're 'splashing' the cash, how about investing in water treatment works which convert sea water into drinking water? I understand that this technology is already possible— and we all know that there's more sea water available now because the polar ice caps are melting!

I cannot believe that long-term solutions cannot be found in the short-term to many of the challenges we all face today—but more often than not, there are the ever-present factors of the costs involved in installation, operation and subsequent maintenance— and who will be funding it. Given the choice, I'd far rather pay towards solving future problems now than spend the next ten or twenty years worrying about it. Whatever is needed, then let's get on with it and sort it out now – and I'm sure most people would agree that it's better to pay towards a future-proof drought now, than wait until it's too late and we're facing water rations and not being allowed to wash ourselves and our environments thoroughly, which will bring back diseases from the Dark Ages such as the plague! (A little dramatic but true.)

Thankfully most other things in life require no immediate action but just require rolling with it, and of these other things, there are those enjoyable elements involving wellness and keeping fit if desired. Now, given that I regard housework as the equivalent of a full work-out sometimes, I still try to factor in a blast or two each week on our cross-trainer at home. I don't know where the idea came from but I decided to start playing my old vinyl records from the 1970s and 80s every time I used the cross-trainer; and moving to a disco beat is so much fun and energetic because the 12" singles play for several minutes at a time.

It amazes me how I still feel every beat and want to dance to the music which has been a part of my life since the 1970s. Inevitably my exercise routine had not just been boosted in a physical way but is lifted in a soulful way too. I actually started looking forward to the micro blast-out work-out—without actually putting my back out from dancing!

My music collection is my investment in all things soulful and I would strongly recommend anyone re-visit their times past in this way; to not only keep fit and lift one's spirits but to keep the music alive. Such songs used in my fitness regime include: Disco Nights - G Q, and very appropriately 'Keep Your Body Workin' – Kleeer; yes, correct spelling and the actual vinyl is clear!

I have a vast collection of disco music from my heydays as a disco diva-cum-occasional-DJ. I well remember the anticipation and excitement I used to feel when I'd acquired a particular song or album which I'd sometimes had to order in advance from a particular record shop. To hold my new addition (my baby even) and have that sense of utter joy and fulfilment is no less the same desired joy and fulfilment I was now seeking in a larger commodity of property and way of life.

My taste in music has expanded over the years and now there's a sound for every mood and occasion; from Joplin to Chopin with every genre in between which I can listen to on any day of the week—or not as the case may be. In homage to some of the past artists who are no longer with us, I once assembled their music media from my collection and took a picture, which I not only treasure but feel extremely privileged to have been able to enjoy such music, then and now.

Another unintentional investment I made from the past was to acquire a large number of reference books—mostly home design orientated with plenty of pictures which, although slightly dated in some instances, (since the 1980s and 1990s) are still inspirational when I refer to them today. I didn't have much money at that time but did attend book fairs and boot sales where I found used and new books at a snip of the original price. Whether a cosy cottage or period home, the look can be timelessly classic and stylish regardless of the era or fashion. For me, homely blessings consist of meaningful pictures & artwork, books, quality fabrics, knick-knacks, plants and even a pet or two (or five) around the place. I'm reminded that my current surroundings are very important to me because they reflect the person I am; and wherever I live, they will be the same important source of comfort and companionship to me—as indeed will my husband, of course. (Oh, and not forgetting the 'rabbit hutch' cabinet!). It was so called by Tony and was an auction find many years ago when I lived alone and I've become even more attached to this useful cabinet over time, so will never part with it.

Back to reality and just days before we were due to go away, a letter arrived from the car dealership where we'd purchased our car a number of months before, to say that our car was being 'recalled'. My immediate reaction was to postpone our plans and sort this issue out immediately.

Tony was not so fazed about it but called the garage and, after explaining about our long journey in a few days' time, was assured that the recall was purely precautionary and to continue with our plans but to bring the car to them the following week. The proviso being that we take their phone number and contact them should there be any problems whilst we were away.

I wasn't too pleased because now I was aware that our car had a potential problem, so I wasn't about to ignore it. We'd had no problems with the car so far and so I would just trust that all was fine and wait until we returned from our trip before complete peace of mind would be restored.

Isn't it typical that these things happen and just before you're planning a trip! Not surprisingly, I had a restless night of little sleep and at four a.m., I saw the telephone light on which suggested a problem. Then the light went off, together with the street lights, because there'd been a power cut. It probably wouldn't make too much of an impact at four a.m. but how long the power cut would last, was anyone's guess. I started to wonder if there'd be enough hot water to shower in the morning. We wouldn't be able to boil the kettle for tea either, let alone have toast so we'd have to go and have breakfast at the nearby hotel. I had it all worked out but dreaded actually carrying out all the procedures. I consoled myself with thoughts that at least it would soon be getting light and the temperature in the house was mild enough for us not to need heating.

After an hour or so, the phone gave a single bleep which indicated that the electricity was back on (yay!) and in due course I got up and fed the cats, made tea and toast and extended the timing for the hot water so I could wallow in a hot bath. I reminded myself that inconveniences happen all the time, to all of us.

And so came our trip to the west country. This time there was less uncertainty involved because we were to be taking the same route, to the same town and staying at the same hotel for two nights again, on a dinner, bed and breakfast basis. The other similarity was that my suitcase bulged again with too many jumpers packed inside and so another two 'overflow' bags were essential with one containing magazines, maps, food, snacks, drinks and the important printouts of the favoured property details we'd arranged to view. I've never managed to travel light; it's a mystery to me!

Unlike the last time, I wasn't feeling as overwhelmed by the whole process of vast travelling and scale of the massive lifestyle change we were seeking. No, this time I felt a sense of adventure and excitement at the prospect that this time we might actually be finding our forever home at last.

Our cats were in the safe hands of our next-door neighbours who would be coming in twice a day to feed them—although I doubted they'd see much of the cats as they tend to hide when other people come to the house, except Whingey who really couldn't care *who* feeds him!

Although the journey times would be similar – up to six hours each way – I decided against watching the clock and accepted that we'd be leaving our house mid-morning and probably arriving late afternoon having stopped en-route for a break and lunch in our car. Our lunch would be cheese rolls, twiglets and a few sweets washed down with orange juice. Throughout the journey there would also be ready supplies of marshmallows which, for some reason, have always been a must for us during long journeys—and the packet is mostly empty by the time we get back home.

Coupled with my wittering to Tony about the various 'interesting' magazine articles I'd found, the time should pass quite quickly. By coincidence, one magazine featured insights about various couples who'd either decided to rent out rooms in their houses or start a bed and breakfast business—with hints and tips to boot! Well, this was a great time passer and Tony listened with interest before discussing our hopes and dreams in this respect and how we could make a success of this kind of business whilst becoming financially self-sufficient at the same time. It was a welcome and insightful subject which confirmed our expectations. Somehow Tony and I had got over the squabbles we used to have in the car, and we would now just get on with the journey, long or short.

By the time we'd eventually left the motorways with their slightly inconvenient roadworks, it was late afternoon and we were less than an hour away from the hotel. Just like the last time, the traffic petered out, and we trundled along country lanes through pretty villages with the setting sun before us. As far as the eye could see was this newly discovered landscape of rolling hills and fields of green—and sheep with tiny lambs bounding around with their tails wagging like dogs. When our destination looked this good, every minute of our journey had been worth it.

Tony and I felt so relaxed already and kept saying how lovely the scenery was and how it felt like we were going home. The late afternoon sun was a definite blessing and the weather wasn't even cold. We opened the car windows and this time didn't get the overwhelming farmyard smells we'd had the previous autumn! Instead the air was meadow fresh and those fabulous views were working their magic once again with all the promise of everything we'd wished for – the lifestyle, the home and the opportunities – being right there.

Our first evening at the hotel went well, and we had much to talk and speculate about, with the particular viewings we had lined up. The one property which had interested me the most fitted every criterion: A two-bedroomed cottage with an upstairs bathroom, garden, parking and an annexe next door. It had oil central heating and mains water and drainage (a big tick on my list) and was in a quiet location but only two miles from the nearest town which had adequate shops and facilities. It was priced at the top of our budget but was ready to go as either a B&B or a self-catering holiday let.

The property which most appealed to Tony was cheaper but more of a project: A larger Victorian cottage—also with oil heating and mains water and drainage but adjacent to it stood a very large workshop ripe for conversion. Tony was of the mind that we could convert the large workshop to rent out as a holiday let but obviously we'd have to be prudent about costs and time frames because we might run out of money before we had the chance to rent it out.

The other two properties were 'drive-bys' which we wanted to do before booking a viewing: one was a very small cottage at the top of a steep hill and the other was a complete renovation into the 21st century from probably stone-age man by the looks of it! Over dinner we decided to discount the renovation because it was not for the faint-hearted and too speculative on costings. Three potential properties stayed on the list and the next day promised to be interesting.

The next morning the sun shone brightly and the temperature was much warmer than we were expecting—so much so, I didn't actually wear any of the jumpers I'd packed but luckily had some cotton tops which I wore with my rain jacket, so much more suitable.

After a cooked breakfast, we walked around the

local town and popped in to a few shops (well it's rude not to have a browse around after having come all this way!). We saw a few familiar faces from our last visit and struck up conversations which were very pleasant and made me even more convinced that we'd fit in well there.

As we walked across the street, I saw a penny coin and so I picked it up and put it in my pocket for good luck as the saying goes. Tony just raised his eyebrows at me and said we can make our own luck. Strangely enough, later that day when we'd returned and had gone for a walk before dinner, we saw a black cat appear on a wall on that same road and jump down to run across the road right in front of us—well what another lucky sign which truly made my day.

However, the three viewings went something like this:

We decided to explore the 'drive-by' property first as it was on the way to our first actual viewing, being the cottage with a purpose-built annexe. So up a narrow single track we drove, up and up and up. How we would manage with a removal van was anyone's guess but alas, it couldn't happen anyway because the cottage was tiny, and I certainly couldn't see us living there with five cats. A lovely spot though with magnificent views which probably explained the price. We both agreed it wasn't worth contacting the selling agent and so continued with our plans.

On we drove for another ten miles or so towards the cottage and annexe that I had been particularly keen to see. On paper it had everything we were looking for and a small dark kitchen with lots of greenery outside—in fact, the pictures had reminded me of the time in our old house when Tony and I had the same spooky moment in different rooms of the house because I'd envisaged cooking in a small dark kitchen with lots of greenery outside and Tony had said he'd been changing the bedding in another house. It was as if we'd both been shown a portal into another time and place. I'd been stirring gravy on the cooker and suddenly felt transported elsewhere to a small, dark kitchen and yet I felt calm and blissfully happy. Tony had been upstairs changing the bed (which he doesn't normally do) but seemed definite in his account of being in another house at that same point. However, when we arrived at the cottage and went inside, I felt quite deflated. It was a lovely cottage without a doubt, with inglenook fireplaces and a quirky character about it. The ceilings were not too low, and Tony managed to walk around without ducking his head to avoid the old wooden beams, so no problem there. The upstairs bedrooms and bathroom were fine and indeed the adjacent annexe and garden beyond had everything going for them. The agent was showing us around and we looked around twice but said very little. However, I just didn't feel a connection to the place at all. Tony said afterwards that he couldn't see us living there and it was all a bit too higgledy-piggledy for his liking. So that was that then.

The next viewing was half an hour's drive away, and we drove up and down many hills and fields where sheep stood at the side of the road, staring at us as we slowed up and stopped, before they crossed! It was as if they were looking at us to see whether we would stop or not! This happened a few times and the little lambs would then follow their mums across the road as if to know that mum had to stop the traffic first. It would figure that the flock are streetwise and that's why they're left to their own devices—plus there wasn't much traffic to contend with anyway. Some of the scenery was breathtaking and above us we saw huge birds soaring high in the sky; they were red kites, we were told. There was a time not so long ago when I would never have considered living anywhere so wild but now I was very interested to see what properties and lifestyle were available there.

After suddenly passing a few properties, a post office, shop, community hall and pub, we pulled up outside a rather tall and imposing Victorian cottage—much taller in real life than the pictures showed and with original sash windows by the looks of it. Next to the house was a huge workshop which appeared in obvious need of complete renovation, including the roof. A friendly couple welcomed us in, and I immediately felt a strong connection to this very special home. There was nothing fancy about it: a basic and small kitchen, two large reception rooms and two bedrooms upstairs with a separate bathroom. Through the huge windows lay the most magnificent views of hills and fields with a few other houses dotted around. It was absolutely amazing and to know that there were local facilities close by was yet another plus point. At that moment I was coming to the realisation that this was happening for real and we could actually be living in the very house and following our dreams, pending the assessment of that workshop. There was also a small wraparound garden which was perfect in terms of being low maintenance and the cats would have plenty of room to roam in the surrounding countryside. We then went in the huge workshop and although it had mains water and electricity connected, I couldn't help but see the vastness of money that would need to be spent just to adapt the building and make it suitable to rent. It would take tens of thousands of pounds and goodness knows how long the renovation would take, but I wasn't going to burst any bubbles before talking it through with Tony. We thanked the couple very warmly and said we'd be in contact with the agent when we'd made a decision.

As this viewing had been early afternoon, we'd taken some sandwiches we'd purchased from a shop that morning so we stopped at the side of a road not too far from the house and spent the next half an hour or so eating and talking about all the possibilities pertaining to that house. Tony said he'd felt that connection too and it certainly confirmed to us those intrinsic feelings not only exist but are crucial in finding a forever home. The two fundamental factors which kept our feet firmly on the ground were that we hadn't yet sold our house so we'd have to reduce the price if we wanted to speed up the process, and also that the costs of that renovation quite possibly could exceed our budget and render us completely broke. It was a classic head-and-heart situation and we both felt the same love and concern for the same factors. By the time we'd discussed it for the umpteenth time over dinner that evening, we were coming to the conclusion that we would not be putting in an offer on the house. How could we when we were not a position to move anytime soon let alone start a building project with limited funds? If it had been the other way around and we'd fallen for the first cottage, we could have at least asked if they'd be prepared to wait until we'd sold our house.

Strangely enough when we started our journey back home the next morning, we both felt a sense of getting closer to our dream. Even though we hadn't nailed it on this occasion, we still came very close. I know that 'almost and not quite' might as well be a million miles away but I found the whole experience very encouraging and whilst I didn't feel it was necessary to reduce the price of our house just yet, I was sure the year will continue to be insightful.

I have mentioned before about the significant years in my life which have occurred every twenty years plus three years after that.

1978 - I left the family home in Kent and moved to London.

1981 – Following my job relocation I moved to Essex.

1998 – After a scary wake-up call, I changed my life.

2001 – I fell in love and married.

2018 – I found the perfect place where I'd like to live.

2021 – A final move to my Forever Home?

These are the years when major events occur; such as moving house, getting married, starting jobs, leaving jobs – and having my emotional awakening, which changed my life forever. In 2018 I was half expecting one of these noteworthy events to take place and I did find a very special place, which might be where I'll live one day. However, for most of 2018 we needed to care and support our dear cat Issy and help her recover from a terrible illness. I wouldn't have changed our helping her for anything. She made it through.

Everything just felt like the right thing to do. So actually, 2018 was true to form and did deliver as one of the most influential years of my life. The next significant year in the pattern is 2021. I'm not saying that I'd deliberately wait for a particular year before making any life changes – and I'm certainly not ruling out 2020, but this is how 'synchronicity' is rolling out and if it is the case, I'll most likely be writing about it too. I look for patterns so watch this space. I'm not sure what will be happening in between times but whatever it is, I'll be rolling with it as best I can.

Chapter 3

Catapulted

As the merry month of May arrived – all too quickly – we had a sudden call from the agent to tell us someone wanted to view our house. Once again, we rushed around for a few hours in order to get the house looking its best and then waited for the knock at the door.

A very pleasant and confident young couple came through the house whilst mentioning that they had several properties to see that day. It would figure that it really is a 'buyers' market' at the moment with much on offer but we ourselves are not in a position to make offers elsewhere until we've sold ours—after all, who wants to accept an offer on the basis of then waiting until that buyer's property is sold? We didn't have the background information on this couple but would have needed to know their situation if an offer was made.

A few days later the agent called and said that whilst the couple loved the house, it wasn't for them. Fair enough – we did all we could even though we'd promised not to rush around again – we still did and still will next time.

The start of our new 'wish list' of properties

online was also a disappointment because they all eventually showed as 'under offer'. This whole house move process was even more unpredictable than I had anticipated, and it was tempting to just give up on the notion of selling ours that year (again). We couldn't *make* people buy our house and we couldn't make offers on other properties either; if the time's not right, the time's not right. So, we decided to keep the situation as it was until the end of May and then consider removing our house from the market and waiting until early the following year. Everything would hinge upon the situation at the end of May.

In the meantime, I had the perfect diversion for my attention which was sort of helpful to our situation too: I'd seen an article in a magazine about a 30-day challenge to declutter. Now, I have had many a quick blitz on putting a handful of rubbish in the bin and taking a bag of clothes to the charity shop. But this was a bit different. How it works is this: Day 1 – throw one item away. Day 2- throw two items away, Day 3 – three items and so on, so that by the time the 30 days is up, 400 items would have been cleared from the house. I thought I'd give it a try and if necessary, give up at the point of twenty-plus items. Well I have to say, it was a great way to declutter because I found myself searching and focussing on the number of items to get rid of and it's amazing how many faded, worn, cracked, tatty, chipped, cracked, unwanted or almost unnoticed items can be found! Out went such things as coaster mats for drinks—so many were worn and faded. Some plastic storage boxes contained things like hoover tools which we never use and actually I think some tools were from a previous hoover so out they went and some of the plastic storage boxes too because they were tatty as well. Now I'm not advocating an increased contribution to landfill sites, but if any items were not good enough for the charity shop or to be given to the people we know, then in the bin or on the bonfire they went, sorry.

I reached day twenty and had thrown away some really old jumpers in my count and tidied the wardrobe as a result. It wasn't only therapeutic but also provided me with a feeling of seriously preparing for new times ahead. I also sorted through piles of old photographs some of which had scenery I didn't recognise, or other pictures were out of focus so actually around 100 photos also went on the pile for the bonfire.

Tony mentioned that some stuff could be used for packing material but that would only mean discarding it at the other end, so I said I'd rather use existing clothing and fabrics for packing. So, as Tony is very much into decluttering, he started contributing to the daily number of items too, with pleasure.

During this time, we received surprise invitations to a few celebrations of family and friends which also required overnight stays. We asked our neighbours if they could look after our cats again and they were pleased to help so yes we could get out and about again and I could reacquaint myself with life and social interactions for a while—but I felt I might need a new outfit after all my decluttering!

Until then, I resigned myself to the fact that it was to be a while yet before we would ever leave this house; a year or two maybe because these things do take time and I've no doubt that the longer our house is on the market, the less appeal it will have to potential buyers. I know this because we have seen houses for sale for several months and ask ourselves, "Why hasn't it sold?" The question is: did we really want to take the house off the market and wait until the following spring? In my mind, the answer was 'no'. I wanted to move away and that wouldn't happen at all if the house is not for sale.

How ironic that my books are based upon the following and trusting of one's own instincts in search of finding that inner feeling of complete peace, amongst like-minded people, when in fact, I am far from proving that this theory actually works! Seriously, I've been out of work for four years now and am fortunate to have a private pension payment each month which, coupled with my efforts in housekeeping and gardening, equates to a mutual contribution to the proverbial matrimonial table – in my opinion. Yet there is a self-induced suspension of life as well; a lack of purpose in the daily drudge of routine because I am waiting. Waiting for the house to sell, waiting to move to another county where a new life can begin and where a new business opportunity can take effect.

All these thoughts were hypothetical of course but the one thing I did know is that my future didn't start here. If it weren't for the cats and their personalities for company, I think I might start to lose sight of having any future at all. Their constant attention towards me – and to Tony when he's home – is very genuine and uplifting. Just to see Issy playing around the lounge with her toys, throwing them in the air and jumping on them when they land is a reminder of how important our cats' happiness is to us—and indeed their welfare. I take no comfort from knowing that they may be uprooted in the near future but when that time does come, it will be to a new and better place for a better life together—all of us, happy and healthy.

In the final week of my decluttering (of which I was very proud) I decided to bring my life of pigeonhole tasks back to normality. I hadn't seen any friends for a while and so decided to send a text to some friends of ours to ask if they wanted to come over in two days' time for an afternoon cup of tea and piece of cake. It was the middle of a Tuesday afternoon at the time and so I thought I'd invite them for Thursday if they were free. I sent the text, but my phone bleeped a 'failed' message. That was strange since I had full power and signal. I tried again; the same happened. I tried my friend's husband's number; the same happened. They couldn't have both changed their numbers, surely? I sent the message to my own phone. Still the same response. Now, anyone who knows me or has read about my relationship with my phone will know that I've had some very spooky things happen with it like having a text (which I sent) return on my phone ten years later. I'd also had random messages relating to the family and so I put this particular scenario down to it being a sign not to invite my friends round on Thursday. Fine.

However, it didn't alter the fact that my phone was getting old; at least twenty years and as much as I loved it and looked after it as best I could, age and vulnerability were clearly prevalent as well as that spooky way it talked to me sometimes because the very next day it was working perfectly well. I'd had calls on it and exchanged texts on it but then disaster struck: it fell out of my trouser pocket when I was cleaning the floor but still showed as working by the signal and power band. I thought I was lucky but later realised that the ringer wasn't working, and the texts and calls were just vibrating... my phone was dying. Sorry to sound dramatic but that was the sad truth. I was gutted.

When Tony arrived home from work, he took the back off the phone and rattled it around a bit but no joy, still the same. He took all the casing off and then tried to switch the phone on—nothing. It wouldn't even switch on now. My phone, my pride and joy, had officially died. :(

With all the clearing out I had been doing, this was certainly time to consider upgrading to a new phone but I had a better idea: If I could get a reconditioned phone the same as mine, I could swap the SIM card and outer casing and voila, I could effectively have my phone back again—well the inside and outside at least. The middle bit can rest in peace in my trunk of special memorabilia.

I looked online and found a reconditioned phone exactly the same as mine (I hoped that someone hadn't used it for long before they upgraded to another phone) and so I quickly purchased it and had the response that it would arrive here in the following week or so. *Fingers crossed*, I thought. In the meantime, I went to the cupboard and found a very old spare mobile phone (not similar to mine) but useful nonetheless as I could swap my SIM card temporarily. Although the phone hadn't been used for a few years, I was surprised to see that there were still a few bars of power left on the device but felt it necessary to recharge it beforehand. Now here's a thing: where's the phone charger? I hadn't seen it in all my decluttering and although Tony managed to unearth the box for the phone, there was no charger inside. Aaaaarrrrgh! Why is life so complicated sometimes?! No other charger would fit this phone and so I had to do a house-hunt to search for it with help from Tony who was busily rooting around in the garage.

I remembered a few boxes I'd squirrelled away upstairs in cupboards, which I had packed earlier in the year year with incidentals like fridge magnets and small pictures. I'd bound them in tea towels and bubble wrap. I now carefully rummaged around in one particular box and found a pair of sunglasses I thought I'd lost (oops) then I saw a black 3-pinned plug with cabling wrapped around it; it was the battery charger for the phone – yay! How ridiculous that I should get so excited about such a scenario but there we are. I yelled out to Tony that I'd found the charger and he just smiled and raised an eyebrow just like he always does whilst a small dimple appears next to his mouth. It's a unique look which says, "I'm not saying a word."

It's a look which I know and love.

Without further ado, the temporary phone was

up and working again and sure enough a few days later the replacement phone arrived. I wasn't expecting perfection, but the phone had one button which wasn't fully functional and there was a small crack on the corner of the phone, so I had to contact the seller and ask for another replacement. I received a reply to say they'd send a replacement with a self-addressed envelope for the first one to go back. Fine, so far so good. A few days later the replacement phone arrived. It too was faulty because the screen light was quite dim and the space bar (0) on texting wasn't fully functional so texting was very frustrating. Back to the seller again I went with the request that they either send a replacement that they'd checked beforehand or they refund my money and I'd return these two phones. They replied quickly: Return both phones for a refund. No apology, no niceties. I sent both phones back and duly received a refund.

I ordered another phone from another seller which was to be my last chance at getting the situation back to having a working phone which looked just like my last one. I shall regard this situation as concluded and will not mention it again… unless I have to.

All this frenetic activity continued: It had been less than six weeks since our last trip away to view houses and already we were thinking about planning our next trip. We had a few properties on our wish list already but knew we needed more to make it worth our while so there was no indication that we would be catapulted anywhere anytime soon. However, Tony mentioned a sensible option of a property he wanted me to look at online. A project indeed but at a snip of our budget so we should have ample funds left and the time to get the place up and running. Everything he'd said made sense to me so I looked online at his property project and saw nothing more than a tumbledown shack in the middle of nowhere which, in my opinion, would be better off being demolished and then re-built from scratch. I was not only disappointed but shocked that we should have to consider a derelict property in our search criteria. I asked myself, "Is this what it's come to after paying a mortgage for almost forty years? Is this really what my life's work and ambition has all been about? No, of course not and it will never be."

Without wanting to completely discount my husband's well-meant intentions, I decided to look online myself and find the sort of property which *does* present a viable option for us. Almost straight away and to my surprise, I saw the most idyllic stone cottage, set back from the road with a wraparound garden, garage and outbuildings. The property sat within a small cluster of other houses outside of a village and not too far away from a larger town. The cost was less than our budget and the layout of the rooms were such that there was a downstairs bedroom with an en-suite shower room—ideal for letting out as a B&B.

Now I had the chance to explain how I'd prefer one property choice over another without getting into the realms of not appreciating each other's opinions. When Tony arrived home from work, I mentioned the property I'd saved which was still under budget and ready to move straight in to and set up as a business without too much extra cost. I half expected to hear at least one reason why the cottage would not be suitable but instead Tony shouted out, "I love it! That's exactly what we want – when shall we go and see it?" Already he'd printed off the details and was working out how we would use the rooms! His enthusiasm was contagious and I have to admit to being just as excited but let's not forget that we'd seen our 'perfect' place before and it was only when we entered the property that we found that it just wasn't for us—no reason, just that we didn't get the vibe. So, we shouldn't get too carried away this time. Looking at the property would be key of course but first we would need to establish when Tony could take time off work, sort out the hotel booking, ask our neighbours if they could look after our cats yet again and contact the agent to find out if the sellers had found anywhere yet (which would allow us to reduce the price of our house and hopefully find a buyer).

It wasn't even the end of May yet but everything was happening very quickly: Tony could take the time off work (he was his own boss after all), the hotel where we usually stayed did have rooms still available and so all we needed to do was ask our neighbours about the cats, call the agent to ask a few questions and book an appointment to view.

We decided to call the agent first and they confidently announced that an offer on that property had 'just been accepted this morning'.

"More likely they haven't updated their website

yet" grumbled Tony. "Well that's done with as far as I'm concerned" he conceded. I wasn't so sure and for the next few days I kept looking for the updated 'sold' notice on that house, but it didn't show. Maybe they were checking out the buyer's credentials or waiting for a better offer? I knew we were hardly in a position to offer any bargaining power, but I called the agent the following weekend and asked why the house didn't show as being sold or under offer. I was told that a survey was to be carried out before the house would be shown as sold—just in case the sale went 'pear-shaped'. Maybe all is lost on that house then.

During the following week, we both concentrated on our house and garden. There was no denying that there was a general disappointment about life at the moment for each of us. However, the garden was looking vibrant with fresh green foliage from plants and trees—and oak apples appeared on the trees this year. I hadn't noticed them before and wondered what the round pink spongy looking things were all about: Apparently wasps insert their eggs into oak shoots which then develop into these apples to protect and nourish the larvae. Yet another example of how nature cares in so many ways, but not all: take the leaf miner moth whose larvae attacks the leaves of its host, such as the horse chestnut tree, causing long-term damage to the tree's growth and reproduction. We do have a beautiful horse chestnut tree in the garden which fortunately, doesn't show any signs of leaf attack or illness.

The final days of May consisted of a plethora of difficulties bringing relentless demand on our finances, communication and patience. Apart from the house situation not moving and my mobile phone palaver, there came an unexpected telephone bill which although was supposed to encompass a whole package of TV, phone, broadband and mobile for a fixed price monthly, had somehow increased by another £30 to the cost (not usage). We tried to call the provider but without success so this would be a case of me trying again throughout the week to see if I could get a replacement deal—again. It is one of those things in life these days when good deals exist but are never offered to you as an existing customer, instead you have to search and threaten to cancel the contract in order to keep your finances in some sort of consistent order. After a number of hours and telephone conversations with the company, we acquired a new and cheaper contract.

At the same time as the telephone scenario, there came an email notification for Tony to check his tax bill which needed to be paid in several months' time. It seemed a long way off but when Tony checked, the amount, it was much more than the previous year and so we would need to save money each month in order to pay it. Tony wasn't at all pleased. I wasn't exactly thrilled myself but what can you do?

My efforts to carry on as usual whilst trying to be upbeat about things backfired and I found myself targeted by unwarranted criticism and further verbal abuse.

There is no point in relaying the specific onslaught of unkind words but I ended up saying to Tony "I think we're done here; I think we've reached the end of the road. We'll get the social celebrations and interactions out of the way, then..." I didn't finish my sentence but left the breakfast table and went to get ready as I needed to go food shopping.

I couldn't believe what I had actually said, and my heart was still racing whilst my mind was saying, *OMG what have I done?! Too late now, I've said it.* A while later I heard the coffee machine whirring away downstairs and wondered if I might get a cup of coffee with an apology? Or maybe not—in fact, most likely not! I hadn't been aggressive but calm and concise, I thought.

At last I heard Tony climbing the stairs. He handed me a cup of coffee and apologised for his words and behaviour which he said he didn't mean at all. He said that I shouldn't say such things either because we hadn't come this far, just to throw it all away. I admit to feeling an overwhelming sense of relief and agreed that we shouldn't lash out at each other either just because life doesn't go our way sometimes. We called a truce and for the next few days, spoke to each other in a very civil fashion— which suited me fine. Tony is my best friend and I don't want to hurt or lose him.

Let's move on with the necessary grit and determination to make life a success and without doubts or money worries.

The weekly food shop should have been a pretty uneventful occurrence but not this time because I was asked to pay £50 more than the shop actually amounted to. It was only when I produced my card to pay, that the price reduced to the correct price. "Is it more expensive if I pay by cash then?" I said questioningly.

"No, I, er, scanned a few things in more than once but I've removed them from the total now," came the answer. I checked the receipt before I left the store and noticed that there were no double entries or corrections shown at all. A systems glitch or potential con? I don't know.

During this time, Tony had purchased two sun loungers for us to use in the garden (when do we ever get to sit outside and do nothing?!) Maybe this would be a good incentive, but I did wonder why he was splashing out at the moment. However, the sun loungers arrived and looked fine: a dark grey canvas seating with a springy lattice edge secured by individual semi-circular welds (yes, it is important that I describe them). So, for a few hours on one day we sat and lounged in the back garden in the sunshine and shutting our eyes, imagined we were on holiday beside a sparkling swimming pool. Bliss. Quite typically, the clouds moved in and so we packed up the loungers for the day but promised we'd use them again the next morning which we did. Except Tony hadn't yet sat on his lounger before mentioning that he'd just noticed one of the welded stays had come adrift on one side. I looked and saw the breakage and suggested that he secure the springy cord with a cable tie around the frame because it was only near his knee so wouldn't notice too much.

"It's not near my knee" he said, "it's here" and pointed to a breakage on the other side near his back!

Two breakages in less than one day's usage. Hmm. "Did you check the weight allowance?" I smiled.

"Of course I did and I'm well within the maximum weight limit thank you!" he smiled back.

I imagined him sitting down and falling through it! But whilst I was laughing, I tentatively looked around my own seating area and noticed one of those welds had also broken! They would both have to go back, and Tony took no time in sending an email regarding a refund before packing them back up in the original box ready for collection.

Standards do slip as we've found of late, but times change, and needs must...

It was clear to me that I wasn't going to be catapulted to anywhere any time soon and so I carried on with the usual weekly search of new properties online to add to our wish list so at least we would have something to see if it was still available, for when we next went on another trip to the west country. Tony also looked online and so between us, we started getting quite a collection of properties in various shapes, sizes and degrees of renovation or B&B potential.

For me, the ideal time for our next trip would be late summer because firstly, it would give our house more time to sell – and we'd probably reduce the price by then too – and secondly, there'd be less holiday traffic on the roads and so our journey times and hotel booking availability might be slightly improved. This was what I envisaged as being the best possible time and outcome. So bring it on!

Chapter 4

Salvation

At the beginning of June, we received some welcome news: Tony was given all the details about his private pension with facts and figures he was eligible to, later in the year. We then calculated this income, together with my pension payment, as our basic monthly income when we moved towards retirement. The amount certainly wasn't something to sing and dance about, but it did mean that we would have some sort of guaranteed income to live on until we could fashion some sort of holiday business into the equation.

This was all part and parcel of deciding to move to the country in favour of a simpler and quieter life, and one which we'd both like the chance at making a success of. Just having this information was uplifting enough to prompt a very serious discussion about our future together—and the inevitable disciplines required in order to avoid overspending on non-essentials.

Finances aside, there's nothing like being reminded about what's really important in life, and that's our health: Tony had started to struggle with walking and sitting, complaining that his back hurt. Well, he had been busy with gardening recently and so I wasn't too surprised but after the third day without improvement, Tony saw a doctor – actually a nurse – who said he had sciatica and said he should take prescribed tablets for a week. It was a relief to know that it wasn't anything more serious but it also meant that Tony couldn't go to work or drive or do much of anything really except sit around resting or walking slowly around the house and garden to keep his limbs moving. Of course, the cats thought it was great to have a ready-made warm cushion in the form of Tony's lap to lie in—especially Foz who needed no encouragement to snuggle up to Tony most days. It wasn't uncomfortable for Tony either so just a waiting game now.

I was thinking about the two social events on the calendar with the first being in just a few days' time. There was that awkward feeling about whether to cancel now or wait until nearer the time to see if he improved or let people down. As it happened, it was us who received a call to say that the event had been cancelled due to illness, so the decision was already made for us albeit not ideally. I posted a note through our neighbour's door to say that we wouldn't be needing our cats to be looked after on this occasion. So that was that.

Considering this was the start of summer, the weather couldn't have been gloomier with dark clouds, wind, rain and cooler temperatures— it was more like autumn. We had every reason to be a bit gloomy ourselves; Tony in particular given his discomfort and pain which wasn't getting any easier and forcing him to lose sleep, but actually we were both resigned to the situation for now and faring very well. We still managed a few walks outside although a much-reduced distance and with slower steps. Even more time than usual was spent with Tony at home needing to relax whilst I continued with my daily chores of cleaning and cooking which I didn't mind doing at all.

The unseasonal weather prevailed and as a result, Tony and I became more entrenched with our individual ways of passing the time – Tony with his TV: sport, films and computer games and me in the kitchen attempting another recipe challenge of the cake variety whilst listening to music CDs such as Andy Burrows, The Pierces and Supertramp (and it is raining again!). Whether I'm cooking or eating or just engrossed in the moment, I can find the whole experience quite hypnotic. One such memory springs to mind when Tony and I had gone to an Indian restaurant for dinner. It was early evening on a cold and rainy day, and we were the only diners there at the time. So far there was nothing really unusual about the circumstances and we'd ordered our food which had arrived at the table quite quickly; just as usual, we always ordered several dishes to share. We were tucking in and enjoying our delicious food and not saying much as we preferred to eat. At that moment, I felt completely relaxed and entranced with every one of my senses fulfilled and blissful. Apart from the glorious smell and flavour of the food, we were in a warm and cosy setting with subdued lighting and calming background music—just as with so many times before. But this time it was different because the vibe of that place, at that time and in that environment, was in complete harmony with my inner self in that deep pool of calmness I've come to acknowledge. It's never happened before like this and so probably a one-off event, but I will always remember that unique occasion which I'd wanted to last forever.

Now I felt another sense of calm in the realisation that Tony was getting better, slowly but surely, with every day that passed. There really wasn't anything else to fret about at this time. The inclement weather outside helped because who wants to be holed up indoors when there's brilliant sunshine outside? The whole atmosphere was beneficial to both of us at the time and following a comforting lunch of cheese on toast with a piping hot mug of tea, I managed to write a few newsy letters to update our friends and family.

Strangely enough Tony started mentioning his semi-retirement and how it couldn't come soon enough—he'd had enough of work, aching limbs and sleepless nights which now included worrying about money as he wouldn't be getting paid for this time off. The prospect of regular relaxation was very appealing to him. He also mentioned a caveat that he'd still be able to cook breakfasts for the B&B business if necessary.

It's a weird paradox that whilst Tony was at home with me (albeit unfit, immobile and away from me much of the time), I found more energy and motivation to work to my own agenda which included my favourite pastime: home-making with a touch more clutter clearing to improve the overall image of rooms. To this end, I went around the house and removed any knick-knacks which no longer served or enhanced the house. Within a few days, the improvements were obvious (in my opinion) and what's more, I thoroughly enjoyed losing myself this way and being creative. If this is any indication of what life would be like when we were both retired – I say, "Bring it on!" The social side of life was missing at the moment for obvious reasons but otherwise, the lack of external influences and not being answerable to anyone (such as employers) was clearly a bonus.

Further information came through from pension companies regarding the unlocking of Tony's funds in a few months' time. We both imagined that this could tie in with our house move but 'imagination' is all it is without an offer made on our house or even credible potential properties to view.

Plus, with Tony's continuing struggle with back pain, all we could do was seek facts and figures about future plans, without actioning any of them. My mum used to say 'first things first' which meant that whatever you're dealing with, work though it in order of priority and by system. To apply this rule now would mean that Tony's good health was paramount before we planned anything else or 'jumped the gun' to coin another of Mum's clichés! He objected to my rationale, saying that his bad back shouldn't be a factor in our plans at this time. I objected at his objection and insisted that his bad back was very much a problem right now and he was in total denial if he thought otherwise.

If I could elaborate on Mum's little adage, I would say that first things are first and then in conjunction with all the decisions and choices we make thereafter but guided by intuition as opposed to logic.

Just as Tony was sealing the envelope containing his completed forms for early retirement, he turned to me and said, "Look at what you've done to me - you've created a monster."

I wasn't sure what he meant and frowned as he continued "I don't want to go to work any more and I never thought I'd say that but here I am filling in forms to allow me to do just that."

I smiled and said, "I haven't created a monster at all, but I think I've encouraged you to be more free-thinking about how your life can improve—and your eyes are well and truly open now".

"Yes, that's the problem," he said, "I can see my new life ahead and I want it now!"

In any event, it seemed only fair to me that as I had unlocked my private pension early, my husband should do the same because we are a joint partnership with equal contributions financially and personally.

Times change, situations change and so do our perceptions; I can remember in the 1990s being quite shocked at the appearance of TV satellite dishes popping up on houses everywhere. To see rows and rows of Victorian terrace houses with these huge white plates clamped to the fascia and all facing in the same direction, posed a discomfort to me and an insult to all things traditional and pleasing to the eye.

Obviously as time wore on and satellite dishes became more familiar, smaller and darker with mesh material, they became more invisible to me. Likewise, the introduction and appearance of wind turbines, which I have never had a particular problem with as they look and move so gracefully, now merge into the landscape and seascape.

All technology is part and parcel of progress I suppose, so who am I to object? In life there is no rule book so if we can solve problems together (which we've usually created) then what's not to applaud?

On a lighter note and with the same theme along the lines of progress, Tony and I were sitting in our garden recently when we became aware that we were talking louder and louder to each other in order to be heard above the ever increasing din of birds all chattering and squabbling over the various bird feeders hanging from the trees. Just on one single bird feeder there were about twenty starlings making one almighty racket as they fought for pole position to win the most food—and completely oblivious to the fact that cats live here!

"I've had enough of this," Tony grumbled "it's bad enough weeding all the flower beds where the wheat and barley start growing from the dropped seeds, but I'm not putting up with all this noise as well – the feeders have got to go – that's all there is to it!" and with that, he grabbed the feeders from the trees and cut a few more down which he'd put up with string. All in the shed they went with a big slam of the door in his final act of authority. I couldn't blame him at all.

A certain silence fell about the place and a few birds appeared back on the trees looking around for the feeders. Neither Tony nor I felt guilty because there are other bird feeders elsewhere in other gardens, as well as natural sources of food in hedgerows. No, the birds will not starve, and we will not have to put up with their incessant chatter any more (says the person who wants to move to the countryside!)

A few days later I saw Tony talking to our next-door neighbour and so I went outside to say hello.

"Did Tony tell you about our bird feeders?" I asked

"Morning Vanessa," came the reply, "oh yes, Tony has told me."

"Well," I continued, "I couldn't blame him for taking all them all down because the noise was deafening with birds fighting over food – we couldn't hear ourselves think! So, no more feeders."

Our neighbour looked a bit sheepish and then said "Em… well, Tony has given me the bird feeders and all the extra seeds and nuts."

I laughed and said, "Good luck with that then!" it was as if we'd passed our problem over to him but I laughed again when Tony came in later and said, "I told him that the reason why I took the feeders down was because I was fed up with all the weeding they were creating—I didn't mention the noise!"

I was sure no harm had been done with either neighbourliness or on the bird front as I will still continue to feed bread to the seagulls on our garage roof.

From all that was currently going on with us, Tony continued to struggle with back pain and so hadn't yet returned to work. I dare say that a few cream teas with home-made fruit scones in the garden some afternoons, helped to relax us both and whilst we were far from physically ready to ramp up our efforts to move house, we did decide to reduce our house price to attract more interest. It was certainly worth a try.

As far as the properties on our wish list were concerned, well, this viability was to be taken with a pinch of salt because every time we called the various agents to enquire further about what we'd seen, we were told, on most occasions, that an offer had just been made on the property. This scenario was a little frustrating but our plans are our plans and so they will continue as such until we have an interest on our house – and then we can travel across the country to find our forever home. If we still couldn't find anywhere suitable, we still had the TV programme makers of "Escape to the Country" to contact and ask for their help.

Life can be full of disappointment if we look for it: with situations not panning out as intended, experiences not living up to expectations, friends and relatives not acting as predicted, employers not considering our worth and even we ourselves not getting enough sleep or losing enough weight etc. the list could go on indefinitely. So what a waste of time it is to dwell on such disappointments when that time could be spent on dreaming about all the amazing things in life that might become possible—even if they don't pan out, there will always be another amazing scenario to focus on.

A perfect example of such disappointment came when I approached the company who had been interested in my bottle stand idea (the device where bottles of fluids such as moisturisers, lotions and so on, can be stored upside down and so avoid unnecessary waste and also reduce landfill). The company had shown much interest in this product in the past few years and had considered its development and production as part of their new plastics range for this year. However, now with various reasons including the prospect of Brexit, the company had decided to drop the idea and so I had to respect and accept their decision. This didn't stop me from moving on and asking other companies if they would consider a new product in their range and so I now had the freedom to do just that. There is never an end of the road in any situation unless we make it so. Do farmers give up their livelihood because of one failed crop? Or this is probably a better analogy: Do birds starve because you've removed their main food source from the garden?! Of course not, they move on and meet their needs elsewhere.

So, there I was a few days later, scouring the internet yet again in search of manufacturers and retailers of plastic products. I found a suitable company and so sent an initial email about my enquiry.

The next day, I received a reply asking for more information, which I sent back straight away in the form of an email with attachments of pictures, technical drawings and photos. I then waited: Day one, nothing. Day two, nothing. Day three, still nothing. Day four, I telephoned the guy who had originally asked for more information on the bottle stand and asked if he'd had a chance to consider the product. He had and was very eloquent as he explained that whilst he appreciated the attributes involved in reducing waste and so on, the tooling of the machinery required to create the product here in the UK would be extremely expensive. For this reason alone, he suggested I look to teaming up with a company already located in the far east who already had (cheaper) facilities in place to make the bottle stands. The advice was good, although I had already looked at this route, but it was too complex to go into. I just thanked the guy and hung up.

Nevertheless, this conversation sent the proverbial penny dropping even further, making me realise that this project was not really ever going to get off the ground. But just before I really did put the lid on this idea for good, I decided I would contact one more company – yes ONE more – and this time it was a supermarket chain. A long shot but worth a last attempt.

This whole bottle stand idea had stemmed from my dismay at throwing away bottles of moisturisers and toiletries when there were still contents left in the bottom of the bottles. As a result, I'd since been using my prototypes for storing various bottles upside down. But now my thoughts turned towards the patent and the 'protection' it provided for the design concept. I felt that the patent's protection was nowhere near as important as the planet's protection from plastic waste in particular. I would hate to think that the UK patent was actually stopping someone else from going ahead with a similar idea of their own. How many years had I been on this project without a result? Too many. So how about using our existing plastic bottles (which we 'recycle') and modifying them instead by simply cutting off the base by about 5" (after washing and drying) and then cutting strips downwards around the bottle, leaving about 2" from the base. Then stand a bottle in it, upside down and voila! The desired results are there putting all the contents at the dispensing end of the bottle, saving time and money and reducing waste. This costs *nothing* to produce at home and does actually help two-fold as, by *using plastic*, we can *reduce plastic* waste.

To demonstrate my theory, I made a quick version from a small juice bottle and stored my moisturiser bottle in it without any toppling over, so it was free-standing. I created another quickly made bottle stand by using a partly used toilet roll and slightly squidging it to shape before placing the bottle of moisturiser in place—and there we are an instant bottle stand. Sorted. I recommend trying either version (see photos in this book). Good luck. And if I hear from the supermarket, I will write about it here in this book, otherwise, I will not be renewing my patent so there'll be no contravening of copyright or intellectual property if you're interested in taking this forward; you have my blessing. Where the 'greater good' is concerned, there is no room for vanity or greed.

We were fast approaching the end of June and Tony's back was no better. He hadn't worked for a few weeks. His prescribed medication had come to an end—as had his inclination to sit for very long or walk around the house. He was clearly in pain and as another weekend loomed, I suggested he contact the doctor again for further advice. This suggestion didn't go down well and so the doctor wasn't contacted and, as a result, the weekend started stressfully because Tony was in so much pain he couldn't sleep; he couldn't walk very much either or sit at all. It became clear to me that he needed professional help from a specialist.

So there I was on a Saturday morning, going through the list of various chiropractors and osteopaths in the local area – none of which seemed to be open at the weekend nor did any make home visits. My sympathy for Tony was tempered by a sense of frustration that we should have sorted this yesterday when such places were actually open for business. I called one of the 'out of hours' telephone numbers and spoke to someone who made an appointment for us to attend their clinic first thing Monday morning. Just as I replaced the receiver, the milk boiled over on the cooker and burned all over the hob. I'd been preparing some porridge for breakfast since we hadn't any bread – because I hadn't been shopping yet – I'd been busy running around as a nurse, waitress, cook, cleaner and carer and was fast becoming intolerant.

It wasn't just the milk that had boiled over but the old-fashioned terminology that my blood was boiling applied too, and so I sent out a barrage of expletives interspersed with grumbles about last summer being mostly spent on cat care from Issy being ill, and now this summer is looking to be the same with looking after my husband who should have been looking after his back and wellbeing in the first place! Tony was quiet and lying on the lounge floor on some cushions whilst I blustered on and on about him having a slipped disc fifteen years back and taking nine weeks to heal…!

I'm sure Tony knew I was only venting because it's what I do occasionally, but I don't mean any harm and he knows this. I calmed down quickly and switched on my mobile phone—a message from a friend was in the inbox but then I noticed that all my old messages from Tony from before we were married and just after, which I'd saved all this time, were all gone!

"My messages have gone," I said aloud to Tony, "but only the messages from you. I've got all the others but not yours, how strange and why now?" I must admit to feeling not only perplexed but quite guilty: maybe I didn't deserve to have his messages anymore because I'd been moaning at him and so I was no longer worthy of his messages of love.

"Don't worry about it," called Tony, "I'll send you some more."

I was still baffled and consoled myself with the thought that I could still remember most of them off by heart and so I'd just have to remind myself every now and then, to keep the sentiments alive. I then switched off the phone and put it on the battery charger for the rest of the day. The phone was switched off until the following morning. Somehow – and I don't understand how or why – when I put the phone on the next day, the old messages were all back, every single one. I was in love again with Tony and my phone and even more convinced that love really does conquer all.

All I had to do now was convince Tony that everything would be okay; in just a day's time, he'd be getting proper help and to bear in mind that there were currently thousands of other people going through the very same trauma at the moment—and some of them may live alone and were completely reliant upon home visits ("So think yourself lucky" is what I was getting at). I wasn't alone in trying to comfort Tony; our dear cat Foz had barely left Tony's side. It could have been a case of Foz just cosying up for his own comforts, but he not only laid next to Tony but was also hanging off a nearby sofa arm just above Tony's head, looking down at him. At night, Foz would nuzzle up to Tony's face and make little meowing noises like I'd never heard before, so he was very aware that this was not a good situation.

It was a little unnerving that Foz was so attentive, so much so that I wondered if there might be more to this problem than meets the eye. I worried that there might be 'complications' involved here and he might need x-rays and further treatments which could unearth something far more serious. Monday would be a very insightful day and I just hoped we were dealing with something curable.

Until then, Tony spent most of his time lying on the floor, on seat pads from the conservatory furniture, watching television or films from a small collection of DVDs. He was adequately amused, and I have to say, so was I when it came to meal times: Tony couldn't sit up to eat and so would eat his (diced) meals with a spoon, from in a bowl which he had rested on his chest. It did look funny and reminded me of how I've seen otters eating their food, in those nature programmes on TV!

At least he could eat!

After a very shaky start to Monday morning with showering and getting dressed, I drove to the osteopath's clinic which was situated along a line of shops and I was fortunate enough to be able to park right outside the building. I had to open the passenger door to get Tony out of the car because he was unable to do so himself. The osteopath saw Tony straight away and I waited in a small and nicely decorated waiting room until eventually Tony appeared a little worse for wear with all the pulling about and treatment. With another appointment made, we were given the confirmation that Tony had indeed slipped a disc and furthermore, with a programme of physio and exercises, it could be as long as another six weeks before he would be well again.

Back home, Tony called the company office which arranges work for him and explained the situation, saying that he would just have to call them again when he was clearer about when he'd be fit enough to work. I wasn't privy to the call itself but was disappointed to hear that one of the first things they asked Tony was how he was going to manage financially. Isn't that a personal question which is of no business of anyone else? And isn't his wellbeing more important? Tony had lightly dismissed it and said we had sufficient funds, which we did: my pension still paid the mortgage and a few bills, and we had a small amount saved which we could use in due course. Anyone who has ever read my books will know that money is not something I worry about—if something needs doing or sorting then it takes whatever it takes and costs whatever it costs. I regarded this current situation as a potential dummy run of our life together after we'd moved house and would have only our pension payments as our main source of income. Living frugally is no problem for either of us especially when the pay-off is to not be answerable to anyone else.

Over the next few weeks, a daily routine was established which for Tony consisted of his exercise programme, his TV programmes, computer and phone games which were all interspersed with eating and drinking (as provided) and dealing with Foz and his continuous attention and affection. Each afternoon, I made a point of snuggling up to Tony myself (sorry if this is TMI) just for a while.

For me, the daily routine was similar to before

except that I did the weekly shopping alone and completed other jobs like cleaning windows, mowing grass and washing the car. I'd also received the gym mat for Tony which I'd ordered online. Designed for men and their workout, it was quite large and padded but most importantly, it was firm and far more comfortable for Tony to lie on every day.

We were over the worst and I could hear Tony laughing once more at stuff on TV, then chatting with the cats when they'd stopped to investigate whenever they walked past. Our sleep pattern had improved too and the news of my pension increasing each month was yet another turn in the right direction.

After our breakfast of warm croissants and coffee (Tony's were eaten carefully from his chest as usual), I went into the garden to sit and drink another tasty cup of coffee. I felt very thankful that our situation was improving. It was mid-July and the sun was warm but not too hot because of the gentle breeze. The farmer's fields beyond the garden were coloured in varying shades of beige from being scorched by the sun on hotter days of late. There I sat peacefully, watching a pigeon scouting around at the bottom of the garden, collecting twigs – one at a time – then flying up into the oak tree to make its nest. To one side of the patio, in varying sizes of flower pots, were fragrant lavender, miniature roses in red and pale yellow and a few pots of ivy made for a colourful display—not just my opinion but appreciated by the little blue butterflies now settled and staying awhile in the sunshine. In a nearby flowerbed, the other yellow rose named 'Hope', which I'd planted a few years ago, stood at least four-foot-tall and proudly presenting clusters of six or more golden blooms on each stem—a triumph after such a precarious start in life. For now, this was everything I needed in life: fresh air, absolute peace, sunshine, nature, wildlife and beautiful scenery which perfectly reflected my inner harmony in knowing that all my beloved people were content and well or, at least, in Tony's case, on the mend.

Our own salvation is within us all and the more we embrace and engage with it, the easier it becomes to access. For me, the paradox is that the more I deliberately 'remove' myself from a troublesome situation and so not even give it the time to dwell on it, the more control and in tune I feel about my life and inner self.

By contrast, the more I worry and fret about situations playing out in my mind in vivid detail – and usually with a negative outcome – the more discontented I become and somehow disconnected from my inner self and mental wellbeing. I think it's all about being true to myself whilst handling any situation as well as I possibly can, without compromising my own equilibrium. It's not being selfish; it's about looking out for my own interests without having to explain myself to anyone.

This is exactly how I functioned throughout the unexpected duration of dealing with Tony's back problems. After weeks turning into months, he still couldn't walk properly or sit for that matter but spent most of his time flat on his back on his gym mat with cushions at one end and a foot stall at the other to keep his feet raised. From there he could watch TV or play computer games so was able to keep himself amused and was still in quite good spirits after all this time. There were weekly bouts of therapy from a chiropractor and this helped not just physically but mentally too as Tony was able to leave the house and have a change of scenery for a while, and talk to someone else.

There was really no point in either of us complaining about our lot because we couldn't change the situation in terms of fast-tracking Tony's recovery, but what we could do was try and accept that this was life for the time being and as long as Tony was improving in some way, however slight, then this was a good thing and indicative of his being on the mend. It was all we needed to know although the doctor did ask to see Tony after six weeks and so decided that he should have an x-ray on his spine just to make sure there weren't any other underlying problems. We went for the x-ray at the hospital the very next day and were to wait about ten days for the results. This was only precautionary and so I didn't give the situation any more thought until there was reason to.

It was all a waiting game. Tony's health, the house sale, Tony's semi-retirement funds, our new life somewhere else, our new business maybe somewhere else. Until then, we ate good food, stayed clean and tidy, had fresh air throughout the house, and slept moderately well. We couldn't ask for much more right then and instead of thinking about any hypothetical outcomes, I chose to think about what we would be eating for dinner of whether to make a cake or cheese scones for lunch.

The next appointment at the osteopath (it said 'chiropractor' on the entrance door) was the following week. The clinic was in another town not too far away and I could, so far, still park right outside the building so that Tony didn't have to walk far. When we'd been there before, I'd waited there for Tony whilst he underwent various and effective therapies. This particular day, I decided not to wait but to walk into town and browse around some shops for a while. It was a much cooler day in mid-July so having left Tony at the clinic, I took myself off for a walk and to see what I could find.

Well, I was so glad that I'd decided to venture out around the shops—not because I'd found loads of clothes at bargain prices (although I did look) but because I helped to rescue a trapped bird which had ended up in a shop window. I was walking past the shop at the time – a discount store of various random objects – and saw a seagull jumping up and down in the large sealed window trying to get out. There were pushbikes behind the bird and although the shop's doors were pinned open, the bird stayed at the window.

A few people inside the shop seemed baffled as to what to do. I asked if they wanted some extra help and a few nods was all I needed to get stuck in and get the bird out as quickly and painlessly as possible.

I suggested we move the pushbikes out of the way first and then form a gap as a pathway towards the door. I asked one lady if she'd stand right next to the door on the far side to stop the bird from going to another part of the shop. Then we gently ushered the bird from the base of the window, and it sort of hopped out towards the door—and then flew off! It was free again in seconds and we all gave a little cheer. This was far more rewarding to me than buying a new top and when I got back to the waiting room, Tony appeared from the treatment room and said they were very pleased with his progress, even though he was a little sore from all the 'pulling about'. We went home and had a nice cup of tea and lunch of cheese and onion in French bread. Lovely.

During this time of strain and drain for Tony in his recovery process and extra running around for me, I awoke one morning on a real 'downer' and thought about the jobs I needed to do that day such as the housework and shopping; and firstly, what we were going to eat for breakfast. True to the pledge to myself that I would shelve all the hypothesising, I got up and ready then cooked a healthy breakfast of scrambled eggs, baked tomatoes and toast. Tony had continued to improve and had got himself up and then settled in the lounge on his gym mat in front of the TV. After breakfast, I cleaned and went through my list of jobs before heading to the shops for the weekly essentials where I also treated myself to a book—Tina Turner's biography which I was looking forward to reading.

I'd also purchased two lottery scratch-cards (only £1 each) and gave one to Tony – who then won £3 and I kept the other. Mine showed I had won £10! We ate some fresh strawberries with cream and then there was a knock at the front door. It was our neighbour who handed us some home-grown onions and a bowl of blackcurrants.

The day was getting better and better and to top it all, when I checked the email inbox later on, there was a message from my cousin in Barbados with a news update and so I replied straight away.

A part of me knew that this was never going to be a day of doom and gloom because, even before receiving the kindness of others and our good fortune, I'd already decided to make the best of the day and get on with whatever was necessary. This I'd done and slept well for being reminded that life has a way of sorting itself out whether we worry about it or not (first things first!).

Bookshelf door

Cake

Happy spoon

Wooden pictures

Music which lives on

Oak apple

Bottle stand

Chapter 5

Holding The Fort

It was obvious that Tony was getting better, but recovery was extremely slow. He was able to walk around more and even sit down to eat meals but not much else. It sounded ridiculous to be telling people on the phone that Tony could now sit up more and eat his meals like before. I could easily have been talking about the progress of a toddler rather than a grown man!

It had already been two months since Tony had worked and so his problem was much more serious than we first thought—or, in fact, been advised by nurses at the local GP's surgery who had given him the diagnosis without any examination. Thank goodness we took matters into our own hands and arranged for an osteopath to examine Tony and conclude that he had a slipped disc in a particular lumbar area which would require regular and ongoing physio treatment.

When Tony had requested more painkillers from the surgery, his GP referred him for an x-ray – the results of which had still not materialised after more than three weeks, so we took it that there was nothing else to worry about. I know we should call the surgery to confirm the outcome but to be frank, we were both pretty fed up with running around and chasing other people to help us out and provide information.

It wasn't just about Tony's physical condition needing to improve but also his mental welfare which was, understandably, taking a bashing with the constant endurance of pain and frustration. It was quite miserable for both of us, but we regularly reminded each other that this was not a permanent situation and so there'd be better days ahead.

Despite the many 'chin up' pep talks from concerned friends and family which were very welcome, it wasn't a sad situation which required emotional support. Actually, we were coping very well under the circumstances, and I had no problem with carrying out extra household tasks which were usually Tony's domain. We were both losing weight and getting some sunshine in the garden whenever possible, so we were at least *looking* fitter and better which was something we both appreciated.

Tony hadn't drunk any alcohol during this time as he simply didn't want to.

After a few more weeks of physio, ultrasound and acupuncture, Tony was significantly better. We were settling in to quite an acceptable routine whilst keeping in mind that Tony should be well enough to go back to work at some point soon. During the actual treatment, I'd be out in the High Street browsing around the shops and making the best use of time before our trip back home where we'd discuss progress (which was always encouraging) and the latest advice from the osteopath.

In the following days, across the UK there were some sudden sweltering temperatures of more than 37 degrees centigrade. By night it was equally uncomfortable and so we had to keep the windows open in order to get some airflow. Inevitably neither of us slept and with Tony in pain, the night-time became a particular time of dread. I dare say most people were in the same situation and even the thought that people in tropical lands *live like this all the time,* still didn't offer much comfort. Our cats didn't fare any better and Clipsey took to sleeping on the bathroom floor—which was a bit disconcerting when we needed to use the loo in the night.

I also felt particular sympathy for those who had to commute to work each day, especially by train, because I am very aware of the resilience required in order to carry out the daily tasks in the office (or wherever their place of work) after arriving hot, sweaty and usually late, only to face the same prospect for their journey home again and only to do it all again the next day! So for most people all around the world, this was just one of those times when you accept what is, and then get on with it. I myself had that very same attitude for years and years of travelling to work until that fateful day when my inner emotional state fiercely objected to my rationale—and won. The cause had less to do with commuting, work or the weather and more to do with my determination and resilience to do whatever needed to be done without the self-care necessary to do just that, i.e. my life became an all-consuming set of rules which didn't factor in my emotional needs like rest and recreation after an extremely turbulent few years. This is why I feel for people who are suffering and struggling with angst about their life and with no-one to share their thoughts and fears. They see no end in sight.

But yet, like any difficult situation, (and there were a few for us right then) it would actually be a matter of time before we could get back to normal, with good health, cooler temperatures and the essential and wonderful sound sleep that most of us crave and benefit from.

Until then I had to continue my cat-food-safety regime throughout the day (don't read this paragraph if you're squeamish or just about to eat):

I closely looked at the bowls of uneaten cat food around the house in order to ensure that flies had not paid a visit. Every summer, I can almost guarantee that, if there's a fly buzzing around the house, it would have almost certainly landed on some cat food (usually wet food from pouches) and so laid its eggs—usually in a nice neat row. Disgusting I know and therefore doesn't bear thinking about if the cats get there before I do. Sometimes I've thought the food looked okay and just as I've gone to put it back down, I've seen a little square of white on a piece of meat and yes there it is—the batch of flies' eggs. It's all very well giving the cats tablets for this sort of thing but prevention is surely better than cure and so I immediately remove contaminated food and flush the lot it down the loo before washing the bowl out with detergent. Sorted. As flies do not discriminate whether it's cat food, dog food or human food, I do not ever leave food uncovered – ever - and if I am defrosting anything such as meat (I would have usually perforated the packaging beforehand) I will always cover completely with a clean cotton tea towel. If you don't

*already do this, you might want to check your food and pets'
food too and take similar action in the interest of the health
and wellbeing of all concerned.*

Another week had quickly passed, and we were
due for another visit to the osteopath. On the way
there, Tony had mentioned that he would rather be at
home in his painful condition than go back to work
and climb up and down ladders all day, as part of his
job (in risk assessment) especially in this sweltering
heat. This was not what I expected to hear, and it
sparked my initial concern about the near future. The
journey home that day was equally unsettling because
Tony and I learned from the osteopath that a few of
his clients had taken up to six months to fully recover
from a slipped disc.

In any event, we knew we must prepare for the
long haul if this was a possibility. The one obvious
thing with a bad back is that you cannot force it to do
anything that it's not ready to do. All you can do is
wait for Mother Nature to repair the damage (or re-
settle the disc in this case) and be completely
respectful of how much you can possibly do without
causing further damage. It was so unfortunate for
Tony at this time but his spirits were still quite good
and when I said that my time and days hadn't
changed much since he'd been home, except that I
can talk to him now as well as the cats, he said that
his days are *better* because he is with the only person
he wants to be with and talk to. Even more flattering
was when the local news programme on TV was
asking for nominations of 'Hot Weather Heroes'—
who were people going above and beyond their

normal duty to help others – Tony said he was going to nominate me! It wasn't applicable of course but made me laugh anyway.

With such sentiment, I was happy to carry out whatever was required to keep the house running and enhancing any furnishings like the bathroom mirror and tall pine cabinet which needed painting. The mirror was not a problem and simply meant dismantling it from the stand then undercoating it on one day and painting it with white gloss the next. It was, indeed, the perfect weather for drying paint! However, my brainstorm to paint the cabinet was much more naïve. I had also to put an undercoat on the whole thing on one day but when I went to paint it the next day with a cream-coloured eggshell paint, I had to stop in my tracks: Firstly the paint was very thin so I knew it would need two coats or more. Secondly, the paint totally ponged with a really acrid chemical smell which concerned me somewhat—and especially when the paint tin had red warning signs on it and blurb about keeping it away from children! Okay no children here but plenty of cats and Foz in particular was making himself very unpopular with me by checking out what I was doing at every stage. "It's no good," I called to Tony "I'm not using this paint because it's poor quality, smells horrible and has warning signs all over the tin!"

"Well don't use it then!" came the exasperated cry from the lounge where he was lying on his gym mat trying to watch TV. I was in the conservatory and would have preferred to paint the top coat there in case it rained; yes, storms were forecast too. The windows were all open so I knew it would dry okay.

So now I had to wait for the small amount of eggshell paint to dry so that I could cover it with undercoat again and once dry, then start again with the top coat, which I'd have to go and buy.

I looked at the cabinet again and wondered if I should buy another colour other than cream. Maybe a mushroom gloss would look better and give it a bit more character—it would certainly match the bathroom. I asked Tony if he thought that was a good idea and yes, he agreed. The next day I went off to the DIY store and came back with a tin of gloss paint called 'Coffee Cream'. Perfect. Without delay, I set about painting and rolling on this fabulous colour of quality paint (which didn't smell of anything) all over this battered old pine cabinet which I think started out as a book case but serves very well as shelving for shampoos and toiletries. Now I was getting somewhere and after several hours, I repainted again to make sure there was good coverage. The cabinet would have to stay put until the next day in order to fully dry and allow me to clean the bathroom before it could be reinstated in its rightful place, full of splendour and complementing the newly painted white mirror. I was glad it was all over as it had taken longer than two days to paint two objects and then a further day to clean up the mess and clean brushes, etc. but it was definitely worth it. Both pieces looked perfectly suited to the bathroom and colour scheme—they weren't perfect and I won't be embarking upon any upcycling projects any time soon, they were good enough and have brought the bathroom back to life again.

There was a time when my painting projects –

whether decorating or painting furniture – were quick, easy and effective but this time (and probably because I was out of practice too) the extra time and effort involved came as quite a surprise to me and I'm sure that had I known this, I'd have waited until Tony was well again before embarking upon more tasks when I was already running around more than usual.

I think that one of the reasons why I had done this painting was because I wanted to express myself creatively: My painting contribution towards home-making had clearly been stifled for far too long. My tastes had changed and I could easily have gone from room to room with ideas about upgrading and colour-scheming (put to Tony) but we didn't have the money to make any changes, nor did either of us have the impetus, time or energy right then. But being creative is still an important part of being ourselves in whatever format we choose. My writing helps to fill this void in my life.

Who am I to say that if you really want something in life, you can make it happen—by hook or by crook? The reality is that finding a forever home is simply not happening. What's more, Tony's setback with his health was a real wake-up call that our lifestyle isn't down to one person's ability to go to work. Furthermore, when you're heading towards retirement age, it's fair to expect that your mortgage would have been paid off.

Now it was time for me to seriously consider our situation and possible outcome. The house sale could not be relied upon as definitely happening anytime soon and with Tony's ongoing treatment, are we going to be like 'sitting ducks' waiting for 'something' to change or are we going to be proactive and take control? I fancy the latter.

With a big sigh, heavy heart and focussed mind, I closed down the internet site where we had three 'preferred' properties saved. There was no point in keeping the dream alive when we couldn't actually travel to *see* the properties, let alone *buy* any of them! No, the pressing issues now were Tony's welfare and our money situation. We had a car sitting on the drive doing nothing, so it was about time I used it to drive to work and get some more income established.

Just before I left the PC, to share my thoughts with Tony, I checked online for part-time jobs in the local area. I don't know why I looked with any optimism because most jobs were outside of my skillset and I had done all this searching before because this was the original plan after we'd moved to this place. Back then I couldn't find a job, except the one where the job description changed after I was offered the position. Also, we now had our eyes and minds open to the possibility of living somewhere we'd already fallen in love with and so it was very difficult to forget about.

What was, until recently, our pleasure and excitement about the future (which was still there to be had) was now turning to be placing our full and urgent attention on a less-than-ideal situation. As the cliché says: When life gives you lemons, you make lemonade! I simply had to find work if we were to stay put on the short term.

Indeed, Tony and I could have a role reversal where I go out to work (part-time) and he stays at home. This may well have to be the case if he does need several months to recover.

I continued searching online and this time checked out the local authority's website. There were a few part-time jobs relating to sports centres and park rangers (which I wouldn't mind if I knew anything about sports or green-keeping) but then I saw a job for a part-time technician which was not too dissimilar to role I had once before. Could this be a possibility? I printed off my CV and then used it to work from as I completed the online application form right there and then. The form itself took longer to complete than I'd imagined, and it got me thinking about whether I was 'too old' for all this work stuff. But needs must and I continued until I pressed that 'send' button which then immediately generated a return confirmation that my application had been received. The closing date for applications was the next day.

Now, this was where a strange coincidence came into play—and regarding a text on my mobile phone: Just before I completed the online application form, Tony and I had just had a cup of tea with fruit scones filled with jam and whipped cream. I'd made a large batch of scones because our kindly neighbours had been plying us with home-grown vegetables and so I'd returned the favour with various home-bakes.

Anyway, that was that and the application form was sent. Apart from telling Tony about applying for the job, I decided to tell my friend, Jackie, because she too works at a local authority in another area. So, I sent Jackie a text and told her what I'd done and that I'd have to blow a lot of cobwebs away, before I could work again and also speak like a human instead of feline! Asking colleagues if they wanted a 'briffdrip' with their tea was probably not a good image to set, but hey, I probably wouldn't get the job anyway. Jackie's response was lovely: 'They'd be lucky to have you' said her text before going on to mention that she was sitting at her desk at the moment (in the council) and enjoying a well-deserved cup of tea and a cream scone!

Well was this a 'sign' when I myself had a cream tea just as I'd applied to the council for a job, while my friend who also worked for a council, was enjoying the same? Probably not a sign at all but we'll see, I mused.

A part of me hoped to get the job but I was also fearful of not being capable of doing the job. We all know that technology moves on so quickly these days and, as it had been four years since I'd last worked, I expected there'd be more suitable candidates ready and willing.

So, as I'm in no position to dictate how life will pan out for us right now, I'll just have to take various courses of action and then see which one comes to fruition first.

I had no problem with waiting another year or so if it meant that our dream to run a B&B in the West

Country was only deferred and would still happen in due course. I didn't have a problem with Tony needing to rest and I didn't have a problem with decorating our house in the meantime and making it more attractive to buyers at some point. Believe it or not, I could go through the house right now and pick out everything I'm not happy with or find that it looks too dated. Yes, some of my stuff does look dated. I've moved on in recent years and so I must have a home which reflects my current taste and the person I am today—or in fact, who *we* are today, so any changes would involve input from both of us. It has nothing to do with fashion or trends or telling people what we have or what we've acquired. It's about being true to ourselves whilst safeguarding our only investment as much as possible.

I remember years ago in the 1990s, a particular friend was blissfully happy and content in her first home she'd bought with her newly-wedded husband. They had decorated their Victorian home with impeccable style and good taste; placing complementary artefacts in just the right way and adorning walls with strategically placed original artwork to show the house – and themselves – in the best way possible, to create a home to be rightly proud of. A very successful and artistic couple, their hard work and authenticity was indeed reflected in their home, so what could possibly go wrong? Well the husband wanted to move to a new house. That was it. No debate, no reasons just his undeniable *need* that they move home, immediately but also wanting to remain in the local area (due to their jobs).

We all know that in a marriage, if one of you isn't happy for whatever reason, then the other must look to rectifying the problem if at all possible. So, the search began, and a fabulous house appeared for sale and was within a stone's throw from where they'd lived. Lager than their current home, this property had development potential which was ideal for putting their creative stamp on.

Within a few months they'd moved in and were busy with renovations and decorating. However, the husband couldn't settle. He was extremely restless and had trouble sleeping so took prescribed medication to help—it didn't. Night after night he paced around in a troubled state and my friend became more and more concerned about him.

So, one evening, they sat down and talked about what was going wrong with this 'fresh start' that he had wanted. It wasn't even a case of him getting used to living in a new area so what could be wrong?

Eventually he opened up and unburdened his tired mind which had been laden with guilt. He started by pleading with his wife to forgive him then went on to tell her that he'd had an affair with a woman from work – but it was now over and he wanted to get on with his life and start afresh, with his wife – hence the move.

His wife was not in a forgiving frame of mind at all and was absolutely furious that they'd gone through all the upheaval of a house move just to ease his conscience—which it clearly hadn't!

What was even more selfish on the part of the husband, was that if he'd have told his wife about the affair whilst at their old house, she could have either forgiven him or had, at least, the option to 'buy' him out of the house (which she had loved). Instead there was no way she could afford to buy him out of this new house (which she didn't now, even if she could afford it because her heart wasn't in it) and so after only months of moving in, that house was promptly sold and the divorce procedure quickly started. It was so very sad all round.

My point to this scenario is that anyone's decision to do anything is usually personal. Whilst I believe that my situation is completely different in terms of underlying reasons, it's sometimes necessary to heed what's going on with you right now, and then make the best of things until some sort of clarity presents itself. Then decisions can be made, for all the right reasons.

To tread water, as it were, rather than swim around frantically searching for answers, was my current thought process and one that I was happiest considering right then. If I got the job then the house would get a makeover, we would live in greater comfort (and still go to the west country for visits) and when the time feels right again, with Tony is in good health, we can have another attempt at selling the house.

Now here's the weirdest thing: There is always another side of the coin (sorry about these clichés).

Question: Have you ever flipped a coin to decide an outcome, whilst secretly preferring one option?

Well, that's what happened to me regarding the job I'd applied for. No coins involved but clarity definitely came to my mind and I found myself secretly hoping that I wouldn't get an interview because, quite frankly, I didn't want to go back into an office environment, learn a new job, get used to the new way of life and then, a few months down the line, turn back to my dreams and still yearn to fulfil them (whilst inconveniencing everyone involved). There must be another way to bypass the temporary option and stay true to the first choice to move home, I felt.

Tony needed more time to fully recover—and however long that would take, is however long it would be. At least progress was being made because Tony was able to walk again without too much discomfort. We ventured out for a short walk and held hands, just like before; it was a rewarding pleasure. We sat on a bench for a while and I relayed my concerns about the job and our plans. Tony listened intently then said, "Darling, if you don't want the job you don't have to take the job. It doesn't matter. We're going to be okay but cannot stay long-term where we are, so when we get back home let's look at the budget again and see how little we can sell the house for—then reduce it."

This did make sense and considering Tony was still in pain at the time of this conversation, I thought it was a very rational decision to make. I felt determined, there and then, that we'd be moving house—whatever the cost! Looking ahead, we could buy a house that was a little cheaper and more tatty than our usual search because we'd both have the time and energy to work together on enhancements – providing that there was no heavy lifting involved!

Back home, we looked at our costings to sell and move. Then we looked at how cheaply we could sell the house. We could come down in price. Should we come down in price? Like most things in life which start with a thought, a decision is then made, and subsequent action taken (or not as the case may be). A three-step approach like the beginning, the middle and then end of any situation. It's all very well *planning* for events to take place but when they don't happen, what are you supposed to do? Try a different tack. In this case it was a 'yes'; let's go for it and reduce the price of the house. I picked up the phone, called the agent and within half an hour, our house was online showing at a reduced price. Of course, it's not to say that it would sell now but it should, at least, gain a little more interest and, if nothing else, the prospect of selling and moving away was back in focus again. I had seriously entertained the idea of staying where we were, but it wasn't my first choice.

It was mid-August and in contrast to July, the weather was very autumnal with strong winds and heavy rain. The leaves on the trees were turning brown already and the large leaves on the horse chestnut looked decidedly rusty and shrivelled even though the conkers were still green and far from ready to fall. The natural world must be as confused as we are about the unseasonal weather these days, I mused. We all know that it's not Mother Nature's fault, it's mostly ours by our selfish living and disregard for the consequences of our actions. What do we do when it's hot? We put fans and air conditioning systems on; the energy required to do so, generates even more heat—and so the cycle of global warming continues with even more hot air going up which then creates even more rain to come down.

It must be time for some humour now and there will always be some humour to be had in our home:

With Tony's increasing improvement (which was easily identifiable by his lessening groans of pain and increasing spurts of humour) there came a day when I'd taken in a parcel for a neighbour who was out at the time. The delivery guy had said that he'd put a note through their door to say that the parcel was with us. Fine. So, the next day, the parcel was still in the hall awaiting collection. It would make sense to just go and drop the parcel off at the house and be done with it which we had always done in the past but this time was different because Tony was incapable of running around with parcels and I was already too busy. So there the parcel sat for another day. Eventually I saw the neighbour outside so called out that I had a parcel for them: "Yeah," came the reply "I meant to come and get that."

With still no offer to collect it, I said, "Well, take it now," and with that, I waited at my front door and then handed the parcel over to receive a laid-back "Thanks."

I went back indoors and said to Tony that I wouldn't be taking in other people's parcels anymore because, to be honest, I believe they'd rather deal with a re-delivery service at their own convenience; and I'd tell that to the next delivery person who asked. No, actually, I'd go one better than that; I'd get one of those plaques made like the one we have which says: 'NO COLD CALLING OR SELLING' and have it say: 'NO DELIVERIES FOR ANYONE BUT ADDRESSEE ONLY'!

Tony laughed and said he liked my idea and I should get more to stick around the whole of the door frame saying:

- NO TRICK OR TREATERS
- NO PENNIES FOR THE GUY
- NO CAROL SINGERS
- NO RELIGIOUS REPRESENTATIVES
- NO POLITICAL REPRESENTATIVES
- NO JUNK MAIL
- NO MAIL ADDRESSED TO ANYONE ELSE IN THE STREET
- NO PLASTIC CHARITY BAGS
- NO TAKE-AWAY FOOD MENUS

That should just about cover everything and might go some way to explaining why we'd prefer to 'opt out' of society to some extent—or to a greater extent! It's not that we don't like people because we do and will always be ready to help others. It's just that we don't like being bothered by wasteful resources (being paper, plastic or time) which are completely unnecessary. I personally love the Halloween time of year but after the first two years of dishing out sweets to children knocking at the door all evening (some of the same groups, calling more than once to get more sweets) we now go out for a meal every Halloween, *and* we take the doorbell receiver with us so that the cats don't get to be bothered by the noise!

So, give me a dream that takes years and years to realise, or indeed a forever home to find and I will give it every ounce of my time and effort to search, however long it takes. Is that a waste of time and resources? Of course not. However, Tony's disability did suggest that we wouldn't be going anywhere for a while yet. Furthermore, given the current economic climate with the effects of Brexit still to ascertain, it would be safer to assume that we wouldn't be selling our house any time soon and so wouldn't be moving anywhere else right then.

The hot and sunny month of July could have easily represented the whole summer season and so it probably wasn't surprising to see August looking more like October with cooler temperatures and milder sunshine in between those showers. Don't get me wrong, I love autumn time with all its dark fruits and smells of bonfires but it did feel typically like that 'closing down' time of year when the harvest is done, and opportunities no longer abound.

I hadn't heard anything about the job I'd applied for (which was as I'd hoped) and the new house price didn't attract the interest we were expecting.

The agent had called to arrange a viewing for a young couple who had sold their house and were looking at four houses in one day with ours being the second viewing. Well, they were a lovely couple with two beautiful children, a little girl and boy who were so excited at being there, running around the garden and screeching out, "Mummy, mummy there's a real-life cat!" every time they saw one of our very confused moggies running past (away). If nothing else, the energy and excitement they brought to our home, was very welcome indeed but Tony and I both knew this wouldn't be a sale because the house was too dated for young tastes and so would need too much money to be spent on it. A call from the agent the next day, confirmed as much. Oh well, that's that then (again!).

My head was getting in such a spin with thoughts about what might happen next. It really was anyone's guess. Never mind the proverbial 'Roller Coaster' of life, this felt more like the fairground octopus where you're going up and down and round and round then back again, this way and that... on and on... it's fun for a while but has the opposite effect if it goes on for too long. I told Tony about how I was feeling, and he recommended that we give the house sale a little longer, just a few more weeks, then take it off the market until the following year and then start again. It might sound defeatist but it was all we could do and, as a result, we both started sleeping more soundly. Peace of mind is evident when you can sleep quickly and soundly. In Tony's case, his lessening pain was also helping—and he certainly had much sleep to catch up on.

As I reflected upon this whole scenario with Tony's illness of three months, which was coming to an end, (he could walk and stand upright with greater ease), I felt proud of myself. I know that pride is not something virtuous (or at least that's what I'd been brought up to believe; that pride comes before a fall) but why shouldn't I feel proud? I'd cared for Tony 24/7 as well as the cats and house and all the other chores which came with that, which I've already mentioned. I could have buckled under the strain or become ill myself due to the stress. But I find that when I'm in charge of something important like this, where others depend upon me, I face it and fight it with all the rigour necessary to keep our lives going as comfortably as possible—and frugally too in this instance. So, I don't think there's anything wrong in recognising your own efforts when the going gets tough; in fact, I think I benefitted from recognising my own self-worth because it made me feel stronger and more able to cope with anything.

There was just one major task left to do for the time being, and that was to take the car for its annual service and MOT. I'd booked it at the local garage for the end of August but a few weeks before the due date, there were messages and signs on the car's dashboard display and I was worried that the car might break down.

"It's only information about the service," said Tony when I pointed out the signs and messages, "you always overreact—just ignore it because it's all booked in to the garage anyway."

Well this advice was about as welcome to my ears as the warning sign was to my eyes!

Under the circumstances, I thought the most important thing to do right away, was to bring the booking for the car's MOT and service forward and incorporate the sorting out of the warning message. This I did immediately and what should have been a straightforward procedure turned out to be a highly charged complication surrounding the car's computer system and some new brake discs. Now I wouldn't normally go into such boring detail and so I'll be as brief as possible: The service and MOT were fine but new brake discs were needed and after several attempts for the garage to override the computer system in order to *fit* the brake discs, the discs were the wrong fit three times because they showed a 'score' mark around them because they were rubbing. It was all becoming quite ridiculous with hours being spent at the garage as they tried yet another supplier for the 'approved' parts. After the fourth attempt, there seemed to be success and the right fit at last. Just as well because Tony needed the car to be ready for work in a matter of days. It had all become a very urgent situation yet applicable to the fact that both Tony *and* the car had both suffered from dodgy discs!

We could have done without the inconvenience and expense caused by both scenarios, but such is life and I certainly wasn't in a position to complain. There had been an apparent run of bad luck and there could have been even more because just minutes after leaving the car at the garage on its last repair, there had been a multi-car accident on the main road, right outside the garage (they told me) so maybe I was actually lucky to have not been involved.

During that same week, Tony had got out of bed in the middle of the night and had gone downstairs because he'd heard a 'loud noise' which had woken him up. I called down to ask what was going on and he replied, "You're not going to believe this but the washing machine *(which was completely switched off as usual)* is filling up with water!"

He then came upstairs and said he'd stopped it by switching it off at the plug socket. It didn't make any sense at all because I never use a timer on the machine and if it had a dodgy water valve, why would switching it off at the plug make any difference? The machine was only four years old but to buy a new machine was all we could do because I wasn't prepared to have an unpredictable machine under my roof, thank you very much.

If Tony hadn't heard the noise which he said was a loud 'click' we might have had our kitchen flooded because I always leave the washing machine door open slightly, to air out. So, depending on how you look at it, we were either lucky or unlucky. The credit card had yet another bashing in order to buy a new washing machine, but it marked the end of our apparent misfortune.

Chapter 6

Charging Ahead

Most decisions I made lately started with either a thought or a gut feeling. I daresay that the source behind either came from the subconscious because it has been scientifically proven that the function of the brain has been linked to the function of the gut and vice-versa. This was all the evidence I needed act impulsively and recklessly sometimes: *It's okay it's natural!*

An easy way to apply this rule is when you can do a favour for someone and even though they don't shower you with gratitude, you know they appreciate your efforts and so you're more than happy to help. By contrast, you might be showered with thanks for a favour done but yet instinctively know that your efforts have not been appreciated on this occasion. Perhaps it's self-preservation or a deep-rooted love for the self but I believe these parameters of generosity and tolerance are unique to each and every one of us. In this respect, it might explain why employment is very much a two-way street with the requirements of the role being rewarded with a salary; and if that exchange becomes imbalanced, a strike or sacking may well result.

Then there are the times when I lack total

appreciation of another's time or effort in helping me and this may be because I sense a lack of integrity or goodwill is involved. Whether I'm right or wrong, feelings play a big part in my interactions and yet, where my nearest and dearest are concerned, those feelings can easily transmute into voiced opinions. This freedom of speech can be plentiful (and colourful) when Tony and I are at loggerheads sometimes. Our choice of words can be hateful and hurtful—but this is only in the heat of that particular moment, often due to tiredness or stress and we do get over the spat quite quickly. I think it's because we operate mostly as a 'couple' and therefore our individual boundaries can sometimes overlap and become blurred. Therefore, in any joint task, we can either be completely united as one or otherwise totally divided; and then the rot sets in very quickly! It could be any situation, anywhere or at any time; such as one occasion in the garden when I'd shouted to Tony over the noise of the strimmer he was using, as he showered me with grass cuttings and mud, "Do you *WANT* a divorce?"

"NO!" he'd shouted back, above the din whilst still continuing with the rain of mud and grass.

"Well you're going the right way about getting it; so take your strimmer and strim elsewhere!"

He did. I could have moved away from the deluge and even been *appreciative* of his efforts but, rightly or wrongly, I sensed a deliberate act of antagonism was afoot (for some unknown reason).

Another more common example occurs too often in the supermarket and, one particular time, went further:

Tony said loudly "For the next food shop, you're on your own; and not just next time but for good because I'm shipping out altogether!"

He'd been moaning after I'd objected to his dilly-dallying with the trolley after I'd forged ahead with armfuls of goods, only to turn around and find that he'd gone elsewhere with the trolley somewhere in the store.

"Good!" I'd answered back "Let me know the exact time and date you're shipping out and I'll mark it on the calendar! And what's more, I'll buy some Champagne whilst I'm here!"

Then we both calmed down.

Neither of us really wants the other to be gone of course but the impression we give, in the heat of the moment when our thoughts, feelings and intentions, completely differ, can seem to be heading that way. We have years of practice at falling out and have grown thick skins and resilience as a result, but we're not out of love for very long. This is probably true of most close relationships and I think that the most important thing is to keep a sense of self-worth at all times and be true to your own values and standards whilst respecting the feelings of others. Thankfully, we ignore each other's poor behaviour and stay united about the better life we're trying to establish.

I accept the occasional angst as being part of married life in the role of a wife with a husband which can transform into a Punch & Judy show – or

Punch & Punch - but without the actual contact. I accept these moments because they're part of the colour spectrum and drama which we bring to each other's lives. Overall, I think we handle our differences quite well and this may be helped by our similar upbringing and ways of handing authority and discipline. We also have similar insights and perceptions about life and general ways of conduct.

As for my other extended relationships with family and friends, they hold mutual appreciation and flow along nicely. They're maybe not as crucial to me because my current and future wellbeing are not as dependent upon them.

At this point I must say, categorically, that if, in the event of Tony and me ever running a business together, our patrons would only ever hear sweet exchanges of professional conduct between us and from each of us—which is mostly, and genuinely, the case.

Now it really is time to move on, not just in this aptly named chapter, but in life itself and so after all the unwelcome incidents of late, a positive, action-taking vibe returned to our lives once again.

With it being only days away from Tony's return to work, which was good news in itself as Tony was fit and well again, life was quickly getting back to a 'feel-good' normal—after three months of suspended living.

Anyone who's had problems with their back, will

know that being comfortable on your furniture is very important, especially the bed. First on the hit list for us was finding a new bed and so we thought we'd go shopping and see what was available (to be purchased as soon as we were financially sound again). The first shop we browsed around sold not only beds but cabinets and furnishings like the mirror I'd purchased once and for which I had received a discount. I knew this was a good place to shop although it wasn't a huge place which probably explained the limited selection of beds on display.

Tony was busy sampling each bed and the varying degrees of comfort they promised so I wandered off and found other pieces of furniture which had caught my eye, like a small wooden dressing table in pale oak. It had a pedestal of drawers to one side and could have easily been a desk. I hesitated to ask more about this piece. As a desk, I was interested but as a dressing table, not really—I've always applied my make-up whilst sitting at the side of the bed and delving into my make-up from a former 'sewing box' where nowadays the contents fix my face instead of my clothes.

Eventually I asked the salesman if they sold desks with a double pedestal. The shopkeeper thought for a moment and said that they did have one desk at their warehouse, not far away, and so would call there in advance if we wanted to see the desk. Tony had been unimpressed by the beds and so was quite happy to salvage something from our trip by going to the warehouse to see this desk—even though it had nothing to do with helping his bad back. (Incidentally, we did find a new bed and arranged delivery for a number of weeks hence). For now, our own desk at home was nothing more than a laminated shelf fixed into an alcove with cabinets under either side, in one of the bedrooms we called a 'study'. For all intents and purposes, it had served as a desk—but was always a stopgap until we'd found the real deal. So, this could be it.

Over at the warehouse, we were welcomed by an employee who was standing next to a rather small and very low desk. Although there was no denying that this was a modern and attractive piece with its light wooden top and painted cream pedestal cabinets, it really wasn't what I had in mind at all.

I glanced at Tony who looked at me, then ever-so-slightly shook his head in disapproval. It was a little awkward because the guy was waiting for a response. I didn't want to just say, 'no thanks' and head straight for the door, so I started making small talk by saying that it wasn't entirely what we were looking for because we preferred the older style type desks, the chunky ones where you can stuff loads of folders full of paperwork or receipts for the tax man! I went on to say that we would continue our search and maybe get a second-hand desk instead – "but thanks anyway."

"I think I know the type of desk you mean," said the young guy, "like that one over there." He was pointing to a dark corner of the warehouse which was dominated by cardboard boxes and packing material. I couldn't see a desk anywhere but as I walked across, I realised that, in the gloom beneath the boxes, stood a very large solid wooden double-pedestal desk—a real proper chunky example.

"That's the exact desk!" I enthused, "do you think we could buy it for a reasonable price?" (They clearly weren't using the desk for anything other than storage at present). Apparently, it had been 'new' some time ago, but had never sold; it was made entirely from recycled wood, too. The guy smiled and said he'd ask the boss.

So, after leaving our telephone number, we left the warehouse to go home and measure up to see if the desk would fit in the alcove. It wasn't the most exciting thing to have happened but, for me, it represented a fresh start where we could then decorate the 'study'. Tony and I could both use the desk in comfort and style. It would also be an attractive piece of furniture to grace our house wherever we lived.

The phone call came through from the boss that we could buy the desk for a few hundred pounds which was brilliant news, but the only problem was, the desk was slightly too big for the alcove—by only 5 mm. If I could have scraped plaster off the side wall, I would have done so there and then! Instead I said that we'd have the desk but would need to rearrange the room because it didn't quite fit.

"We can alter it for you," said the boss, "if you give us the measurements, we can slice a piece off each side and polish it up afterwards." What a star! This day was getting better and better and Tony was as excited as I was. We arranged to have the desk delivered at the end of September as this would allow us (me) the chance to redecorate the room in preparation of this new phase.

There are certain choices you can make which, without realising it, are in keeping with your preferred outcome. The prospect of redecorating again coupled with the excitement of upgrading a room, certainly lit a fire or two inside of me and I couldn't wait to get started. It wasn't just about making the house more attractive to buyers either but making our home even more comfortable for us in the foreseeable future because it was now likely that we'd be staying there longer—maybe until springtime.

I knew this because neither one of us would have opted to splash out on decorating materials at that time or have furniture altered to fit an alcove— although a smaller desk is a better option for the next downsize of property anyway. It was time for another talk and within minutes we'd decided that we'd have to take our house off the market because it was fast approaching one whole year since it was first advertised for sale. We could have forced the sale by accepting the offers from companies who buy houses in order to let them out. They're not estate agents but represent investors in this way so effectively 'cash buyers'. We'd had a few letters from such companies and it was very tempting to get in touch, but my personal concern was that they didn't appear to be regulated by the same sort of governing body as estate agents, and so to me, it could be too risky if the amount you end up selling for falls short of your expectations. Tony wasn't as concerned but said he preferred to use estate agents anyway—so that was that.

With a relatively heavy heart, I called our agent and asked that they remove our property from the market. They were very understanding and said that, currently, the housing market was quite stale with very little selling. We were now back to square one— yet again!

So, there I was, anticipating and visualising this newly acquired desk in our soon-to-be-decorated study of a pale peach colour. I was surprised by how quickly I could shift my focus from selling the house to decorating the house but maybe if we had seen a property which had whetted our appetites, things might have been different.

Tony returned to work for his initial three days a week and seemed no worse for wear except for being very tired when he'd returned home. It was completely understandable.

During that weekend, I got on with planning the revamp and ordering the essentials once I'd run them past Tony who was relaxing by playing computer games (busy in combat as far as I could see but he was relaxing so that was the important thing).

It was mid-September and our particular life and times once again paled into insignificance with yet more global news about adverse weather conditions such as huge hurricanes in the Caribbean (Dorian being one) and flooding with landslides in southern

Spain. Deaths were reported and there was mention of this situation being the 'first time on record' with this type of severity. It seems that we can't stop the weather we have created by global warming, and yet we can predict it to an extent with help from technology—and so prepare as best we can.

Today's technology has also been used to further identify the latest discovery of a new planet (known as K2-18b) and the water vapour in its atmosphere. The excitement comes from knowing that the planet is larger than Earth, is outside of our solar system and has temperatures and water vapour in the atmosphere which could potentially support life. The new planet is over 600,000,000,000 miles away (111 light years) so further research can come in the next generation and may confirm whether (or not) the Earth is unique.

It made me wonder that if there was life on that planet – intelligent life that is – would they really want to be disturbed by us Earthlings? And if, in generations to come, we were to go to that planet, would the (hopefully passive) inhabitants want us lot turning up and taking over, which we probably would, because such a discovery could potentially mean a new home for us humans. Or do we genuinely only wish to learn about other worlds and their ways of life?

It seems to me to be a human condition to search, find and question whatever is of interest— and I am all too familiar with those tendencies. But it also occurred to me that if there were another type of civilisation in outer space and they *were* interested in us and our planet, and *wanted* to engage with us, then they could potentially provide much-needed guidance with repairing our own planet. Even restoring Earth back to health by quelling fires and removing all toxins and waste from land and sea in order to effect future care with today's technology and recycle practices, could help enormously.

Repairing such places on earth like the Darvaza gas crater for example, in Turkmenistan (a man-made accident) which has been burning for almost fifty years. We could then keep our planet this way and so lessen the extreme weather conditions. But alas, this may as well be the makings of a sci-fi film (a bad one at that) but if there was any chance of this happening, it would be in the future for generations yet to come and through their skilful brains, brave hearts and fearless hands.

Until then, I shall continue to pull back the curtains each morning and say, "Hello world, hello sun, hello squirrel, hello cats," (or individual names of whoever I see), and then meet up with the coffee machine, toaster, shower, telephone, computer and radio before getting on with housework as I work towards my quest—onwards and upwards, progressively aiming towards an even better life.

Now to the miniscule significance of my daily routine: It became obvious that neither Tony nor I were actually charging ahead with anything just yet, but we were definitely picking up speed and exchanging more ideas about improvements to our house and the costings involved. Between us we had enough experience with home improvements to avoid those costly mistakes we'd made in the past, such as choosing the wrong colour scheme, wrong carpet or garish fabrics, so needing to do it all again and wasting precious time, money and effort.

Now I am more than aware that if there's one glint of a mistake in anything we buy for the house, then we don't proceed but replace the idea as soon as possible whilst still allowing for compromise in our equal involvement of whatever project, which can only be a good thing.

Now, at least we had the prospect of a higher income by Tony's return to work, fully recovered and free from back pain, then later in a matter of months, when he would be receiving his pension fund payments.

However, the second week of Tony being back at work was a different kettle of fish: Over that weekend, Tony was noticeably quieter and appeared to be unsettled. I saw him flinch a few times as he walked around the house which could only mean one thing: his back was playing up again. I asked how he was, and this prompted a gush of him telling me that he wasn't sure how long he could carry on working because his back couldn't cope with carrying and climbing ladders all day. It was clearly a problem with only one real solution as far as I could see: to give up work now and retire immediately.

We had no choice but to look to selling our

house again and maybe through one of the less conventional methods—to the agents of various investors. It wasn't ideal, but neither was worrying about Tony's back all over again. My suggestion to contact these agents wasn't well received by Tony despite my reminding him that if his back became a problem this time, it may take longer than three months to recover. His plan was that he'd look to working with lighter equipment first of all, and then take it from there. It was worth a try and after ordering various equipment online to ease his lifting of tools etc. he had a few handy pieces of kit due to arrive the very next day. Whilst he would not be lifting heavy loads for his work, he would still need to climb ladders. I had reservations about the longevity of this situation but went along with it whilst continuing my original plan to redecorate the study before delivery of the new desk.

It was the end of September and I was reminded of the importance of respecting each other, especially those in authority, and voicing opinions sensitively without blame or hatred. This reminder came in many forms: firstly, the political unrest in the UK surrounding the ongoing Brexit debate and rather surprising actions and language of politicians in Westminster. There was obviously more going on behind the scenes than most of us were aware of, but it was, nevertheless, unsettling to know that much-respected authorities were arguing amongst themselves about the rights and wrongs of actions already taken.

So too came a global unrest surrounding protests

in foreign lands and the constant barrage of environmental issues being broadcast. I cynically voiced my opinion at the TV screen about the extent of natural resources like wood, paper, fabric, paint and ink, being used to make the actual placards and banners as part of the protest about the environment and it's dwindling resources! How about looking at the bigger picture? I am in no way discounting *anything* that's written because most of it is true, but I do believe that in voicing one's own thoughts and feelings to other's about the environment, that there needs to be respect for the environment and for others – especially those in authority – and so again, to voice opinions but without anger or hatred. No one single generation is responsible for the state of the planet as it is, which has been the result of a progressive and collective mass consumerism by all of us, over hundreds of years. So, if we can voice our opinions and concerns in a clear and calm manner and only concentrate on the issues involved, then we might, as a human race, achieve effective solutions together; and sooner rather than later. Time spent arguing means less time spent resolving.

Some younger activists blame the older generation for all the world's woes but equally, I could blame the older generation and the generation before them— but why would I do that? The generations before me have afforded me my freedom, knowledge, discipline and health by paying in their hard-earned incomes to the Tax and National Health system in order to allow others a good quality of life. They didn't know about things like climate change or even the ozone layer until quite recently and so we all listened to the recommendations and stopped using aerosol cans for a start. Ditto the realisation that car emissions were harmful to health and the environment and so the introductions of catalytic converters came about.

With time and progress, especially towards technology, which is moving so fast these days, there will always be a waste by-product from the dated version of whatever is the 'new and improved' model. This cycle of improvement and consumers has been going on for decades and so it's no surprise that we now have huge amounts of plastic waste which are proving difficult to eradicate. Now the ever-growing population creates more of the same whilst we're still working on the solutions to our current global plight.

Whatever happens, I think it's important to be respectful of others and their suggestions, but what do you do when they're not showing themselves to be respectful towards you? On a very basic level of significance, a particular scenario was played out right outside my house recently which quickly became an issue of respect and consideration. I'll explain as best I can: We live on a housing estate. Housing estates have children. Children play outside their homes. Then children grow up and hang out with other teens on the estate and then the potential to harass other residents can begin.

In our case, we saw a group of a dozen or so youngsters riding around on their pushbikes and then congregating right outside our house. This happened in the early evening when Tony had just got home from work. Sometimes he'd have taken longer to park on our drive because the kids were in his way. However, I just tilted our front blinds so that we had our privacy. There was some noise vocally, but they weren't actually abusive but I did hear a few swearwords now and then (it's just children practising at being grown up!). Anyway, one evening the group decided it was a good idea to hit a football against our garage door and with this, Tony flew outside and told them all to 'clear off' and sit outside their own houses instead! The group dispersed and that was that. We then had a few evenings of heavy rain and so no crowds.

Inevitably, within a week, the group was back, and this time was banging drain covers up and down in the kerbs and making quite a noise. Tony once again went out and said his piece and the group dispersed once more. Then the weekend arrived, and I needed to pop to the local shops. As I got in the car, I was aware of the group again but took no notice and left the drive. They were ahead of me and waited at the junction of a road I usually take (blocking me) and so I didn't use that road but carried on ahead to use another road instead but one of the youngsters saw that I was continuing ahead and pulled out in front of my car (he was grinning from ear to ear, I might add). I stopped the car and tooted in protest, but I knew it was futile.

I got to the shops and returned within minutes to see the crowd sitting on their bikes, on the road, just before our driveway. I had to stop the car again.

This time I put the window down, looked out at the group and calmly said loudly, "Are you all friends with the police?"

A few quizzical looks passed between them before one said loudly, "Yes".

"Well in that case," I said, "you won't mind discussing road safety issues with them and learn about consideration for other road users, will you?"

"Couldn't hear ya!" called one lad who was ripping out the earphones attached to his Smartphone.

"But you still have eyes to see me," I said, "so use them."

The group mumbled between themselves and then rode off but not before Tony flew out of the garage (I had no idea he was there) and said "Oi! Don't you dare disrespect my wife and don't you dare block our drive—or there'll be trouble!"

I felt rather disappointed by Tony's actions because I didn't want this discord to escalate. (It might have been a better idea for Tony to have asked the group to disperse away from our drive before I'd returned.) But now, in my angst, my hand was actually trembling as I tried to get the key in the lock of the front door. Once inside I felt quite shaken up but not due to fear – due to the anger of the injustice of this harassment – yes, harassment which is against the law as far as I know. There have been too many times in the past where my life has been blighted by actions from 'unknowns' and I've been directly affected as a result. This shouldn't be the 'norm' and I, for one, have no intention of accepting it as such.

The next few weeks were incredibly quiet in our

neighbourhood. It was a welcome reminder that this was still a desirable place to live but, as with anywhere, I can only hope that law and order prevail and within this civilised society, it stays as just that – civilised, wherever we live.

In the meantime, I ploughed on with completing the study because the new desk would be arriving in just a matter of days. I'd worked hard and although the decorating had taken longer than I'd expected, I had quite enjoyed the daily round of decorating all day wearing my new cotton gardening gloves to protect my hands from paint. I'd listened to my old cassette tapes whilst decorating, just as I've done in the past except then, the tapes weren't always old in terms of media or artists. So, on went the likes of M People, Black Box and Gloria Estefan and off I went like a well-charged battery-operated decorating machine (if there is such a thing—if so, let me know).

In no time, it seemed, I'd painted large sections of the room before taking each break. The windows were wide open and dust sheets covered the carpet and so after the final flow of glossing the skirting boards, radiator and door, I was finally finished and pleased with the result. The desk was delivered right on time (or should I say, 'ride on time'!) and it fitted the alcove just perfectly.

Over the next few days, all the furniture was back in place and certain pictures adorned the walls. The room had vastly improved from the dingy den it had once been. Tony was suitably impressed and agreed that we hadn't needed to replace the carpet after all (we had seen a new carpet in a shop, only to find that the underlay was almost the same price and then the fitting was an extra £35 – to be paid to the fitter who would be bringing the carpet with him to fit it in the first place! Hang on, the price had doubled already and so we had quickly lost interest in the idea even though extra options and charges had continued to come from the eager salesman). After I'd given our carpet a thorough clean and vacuum, it looked perfectly adequate. The only remaining question was how long would we be having the privilege of using this room? Our thoughts about selling the house hadn't completely disappeared and so this one-room makeover might actually improve our chances of selling.

I felt more in control at this point. It's strange how a simple success in whatever mission you undertake can bring a surge of confidence and optimism into your own being. There was also the payment due from Tony's pension company which he had opted for, three months ago, having completed all the necessary paperwork and identity requirements (which had been returned by post). But now as the weeks were getting on, there was no indication of a pay-out or even a statement or email to say what was happening. It's worth saying at this point that Tony is very laid back about money due to him – except when it's overdue - and then he can get very short-tempered. I work differently and suggested he telephone the company to confirm that everything was now in order and if so, when the funds could be expected.

He was initially reluctant to do this but did make the call a few days later, after which he told me that the paperwork that we'd sent three months earlier had got 'lost' in their computer system. How can it be lost? I wasn't at all impressed, but Tony said that an email from the company with the form attached was to come through shortly and he'd simply have to complete it again then email it back (yes, all sixteen pages of it). This we did and that was that. There was still no news after yet another week. Then came another email from the company asking Tony to complete the attached form (again) as the *other* one had got lost! This time Tony was not so obliging and between the two of us, the air was blue with expletives! The only word which wasn't a swearword was 'useless'! What really riled Tony was that they hadn't even apologised for their inexcusable ineptitude! So, once again, we printed off the form, Tony completed it, then we scanned it and returned it by email (receiving the automatic acknowledgement of receipt); we then trusted that this would be third time lucky: being the third set of paperwork completed and being the third week which the payment was now overdue.

Of course, it's not always the case that customer service can be lacking or poor and despite my lack of tolerance when it is, I am also quick to give genuine thanks when it's warranted. This occasion occurred when I went out shopping for outfits, four months previously, for the social get-togethers—just prior to Tony's back problems. On this particular day, I wasn't really in the mood for shopping and was accepting of the outfit I'd chosen quickly, being navy crepe trousers and a navy-and-cream striped blouse in a similar fabric. The only thing was the blouse had ¾ length sleeves and so I needed some sort of bracelet to complete the look (my watch would be on the other wrist). It sounds ridiculous as I write, but at the time I was getting in a real stew about 'completing' my look but without spending too much money. It didn't help that I had looked a mess that day, having been on a long walk that morning with my hair completely windswept and make-up gone (with the wind!). In my tatty leggings, clumpy boots and waterproof jacket, I felt rather frumpy, grumpy and very despondent.

However, I forced myself to search for a bracelet in each and every likely shop along a High Street.

I was having no luck.

Then I entered a small one-off boutique—so small that the woman at the counter was right inside the door and saw me in my full windswept glory and scruffy regalia. She beamed a smile and said, "Hello." I smiled back, somewhat embarrassed. I could see immediately that many of the beautiful clothes adorning the small space were carefully colour co-ordinated and knew that this was a rather expensive place to shop. However, there was a small arrangement of costume jewellery to one side with handbags and such, and so I started to look at each piece and ponder the options.

"If you need any help, just let me know," said the woman still smiling at me; seemingly ignoring the fact that I couldn't have possibly been her usual calibre of customer.

"Thanks" I said, " I am actually looking for a wide bracelet, lightweight and in a silver colour—and these are pretty close to what I had in mind."

"Well let me see," said the woman. With that, she walked around the shop, stopping at each mannequin which had been carefully dressed with beautiful outfit ensembles, and then returned with the bracelets she'd taken from each of them.

"Will any of these do?" she said humbly, placing the array of silver coloured bracelets on the counter. I saw *the* bracelet immediately which had exceeded my expectations, including the price tag, so I hitched up my tatty sleeve and placed it on my wrist.

It looked amazing and would definitely complete the look of my outfit so I thanked her for her help, paid the money and left the shop with my new bracelet boxed up, surrounded by pink tissue paper, in a little paper bag—handles tied with a pink bow. I left that shop as a different person; feeling like a queen with a smile from ear to ear. I had been made to feel important, noticed, special and valued. That shopkeeper was not going to escape recognition of her exemplary customer care and so, a few days later, I sent a 'Thank You' card to the shop to describe my experience and situation – and forthcoming event which I felt more enthusiastic about – all thanks to her dedicated help. I wished them continued success and said that whenever I was in the area again, I'd visit the shop and, in the meantime, tell my friends about it.

Recently, I went to that same shop – but this time looked more like myself – tidy and smiley. I recognised the woman, but she didn't recognise me. I brought a jumper and, at the till, mentioned that I still wear the bracelet I'd brought from the shop, on special occasions. She frowned a little.

"I sent you a card," I said with a cringe.

"Oh, it was you!" she exclaimed "Thank you so much, we keep it by the till, look!" and with that she pointed to my little card. How lovely. She then said, "It makes everything we do worthwhile to know that our customers appreciate us. We've just started a loyalty card scheme so please take this card for next time."

She handed me a card and had signed for the number transactions I'd made already. I'll be more than happy to go back again and expect that their business will go from strength to strength because they make people feel genuinely welcome and then go the extra mile to help them.

I like to see the positives of life and I believe that the more you look, the more you find—but there was still no evidence of my theory being true on the house front as yet! However, another recent scenario which I think held a certain level of excitement, came about recently when some friends invited us to dinner. We had a lovely meal, interspersed with a few good doses of wine and good conversation as usual. Then the subject of 'antiques' arose. They mentioned a family heirloom of an ivory ball from China. In a matter of minutes they'd fetched it to the table and I was to hold a very old Chinese puzzle ball which was so delicately carved all over with tiny holes of stars and flowers etc. Within the ball was another ball of equal intrigue and craftsmanship—and another inside that one—and another. Five in total all beautifully crafted as I examined and held it in my hand. It was probably hundreds of years old, real ivory; although I agree with the ban of such matter and ways of acquiring it, but nevertheless I was spellbound at that point. There was also a similarly crafted goblet which too was ivory, and the ball sat upon it. I reluctantly put it back in place and asked if they'd had the piece researched at all. "Oh, it's probably not worth much," they said nonchalantly.

Well, the next day I couldn't help but research online about the puzzle ball and found some interesting facts and so I called our friends to tell them about a particular website I'd seen showing a similar ball from a 'collection' which had been associated with the Chinese Ming Dynasty! (doesn't this mean it could be worth a substantial sum?!) To my surprise, our friends waved this off as extremely unlikely and said theirs was probably just a copy. I suggested that they could always send a photo by email to an auction house which specialises in this type of item and provenance. Again, there was no real excitement about finding out more about it. Oh well, perhaps not everyone wants to search, find and question things - and that's fine - so this was a case of the past staying firmly in the past, quietly and unknown. At least it was something I had the privilege to see and hold in the palm of my hand— unlike the ivory coloured castle I'm still searching for and which I believe is out there somewhere and of immense value to me, emotionally.

There was just one property which could figure

as *the* ivory castle—and I don't know why I was even looking online at properties for sale but... it was in the Welsh borders, on a hill, a smallish cottage with a wraparound garden and very nice views of rolling countryside. Not far from a town – which had 'Castle' in the name and the cottage was... yes, ivory in colour. It needed updating in terms of decorating and carpeting, maybe a new kitchen and bathroom but it was typically 'me' in that it was looking to become a home again by transforming its bare, and yet honest, credentials into a magical place to dwell. There was also potential for an annexe by converting a garage and enough space outside to stand a small static home which could be screened off with a section of the garden as its own outside space. Either way, there was the makings of a cosy holiday let as a warm, clean and attractive place to spend time. I saved it to our 'favourites' list.

Now, bearing in mind we hadn't even seen this house for real, we had already, in just a few days, found the perfect static home online—reasonably cheap but perfectly presentable and functional as far as I could tell. It had a large lounge with a gas fire, kitchen/diner, two bedrooms and a bathroom so what's not to like? We wouldn't be blocking any views from the house or neighbouring properties and so it was a possibility; and just as likely as an adjoining annexe to the house would be. Nothing would be possible until we'd sold our own house and so we called another estate agent to get the house marketed straight away.

This time it was a national agent and so we felt

that there might be a better chance of selling now. So, after that call was made, a youngish guy came to our house and was full of enthusiasm about being able to sell our house quickly. We'd heard all the spiel before but sat and listened respectfully until he'd said all he had to say. Then came a rather prickly comment about 'lucky' us for being able to pack up and move away at our leisure and how he'd have to wait an awful long time in order to be in our situation. I just smiled and mentioned that Tony and I had each been paying a mortgage each month, collectively for almost 80 years and that's without the extra thousands of pounds on home improvements so we must be due to a change of tack or a stroke of luck, by now.

Of course, this may or may not happen this time but if we have just the vaguest of interest in our house from a potential buyer, then we are heading westbound immediately to view the 'ivory castle'.

Tony has quite rightly pointed out that we would need to view at least three properties whilst there – and we would for sure – but for now, this is my main interest and if it's meant to be... then so it will. We could then be so bold as to secure a deposit on the static home which seems also to have come to light at this time and even although it's just over a hundred miles away from the property, the necessary transportation and structure assembly are all part of the service.

Things may move quickly and so we were ready for any eventuality even before Christmas, in just a few weeks' time already. My only concern was for the cats and how they would cope with being in a cattery for a few days before a very long journey in cages. This is one bridge we will have to be crossing if and when we came to it. Other people manage all the time and even transport their pets abroad – but our cats are different to the everyday moggies – our cats complain – very loudly – when they're not happy. (hmm, yes, maybe pets are like their owners). But seriously, our oldest cat, Foz, has a heart murmur so his actual health and life could be affected by the stress. Our cats are extremely important to us and provide immense pleasure, so it's only fair that we give them the best life we possibly can. If they were nearing the end of their lives, age-wise, then I would be more inclined to stay where we were for as long as it takes as they live out their lives in peace. Given that they might have ten plus years still to live, then I think it's worth the upheaval for a few days before they have the time to adapt to somewhere new and even better.

I remember a friend, years ago, whose parents never went abroad by aeroplane because they deemed it too dangerous. Only in their later years, after their children had married and left home did they decide that they had 'nothing left to lose' and so booked a flight to Europe for a weekend break. Well, they absolutely loved it; so much so, that they went away whenever they could thereafter.

Fortunately, our cats are blissfully unaware of our future plans and so carry on regardless. Dear little Clipsey (Eclipse) just looks adorable when she sits in front of the TV, looking up at the screen, transfixed as she watches a bird of some kind. She doesn't try and get the bird at all but just watches and moves her head as the bird moves, taking it all in. All our cats have their own personalities, as anyone with family pets will know, and when you have that special bond, it's hard to describe, and even harder to think about ever living without it.

For all our sakes and to avoid living in a metaphorical rut, we must look to changing our situation and move on to bigger and better things. I don't want to wish my life away in the meantime but it does seem that way sometimes: Every time I visit the dentist for a check-up and book the next six-monthly appointment, I wonder if I'll still be living here then but I book it anyway and then sure enough, I'm still here! Three times this has happened, and the next appointment is in six months' time, so maybe by then...?

This is life and with its circumstances and events, progress and development, it's all going on behind the scenes just as is the case with our own personal growth and sense of self-worth. I am all too aware that my thoughts and feelings today may differ tomorrow but I'll always treat with my life with goodwill and honest intentions—with a certain amount of trust thrown in that all will work out well.

Chapter 7

And, Breathe...

After all these months and years surrounding the likelihood of ever finding a forever home, I decided to take a step back and concentrate instead, on my internal forever home which also needs some fulfilment if inner peace is to prevail. So regardless of the late autumn weather with its cooler temperatures and misty rain, I started to tidy the garden of fallen leaves and twigs, which provided some exercise and fresh air. The time would pass quickly on these days—which is always a good indicator of 'losing' yourself to an enjoyable task. Sometimes the cats would follow me and then stay on the patio watching me (they knew that the grass was too wet). This year there was a 'late season' of bees, wasps and butterflies still in action and going about their business.

Being outside was always a pleasure to me, as is feeding the wild birds by throwing bread up on to the garage roof, away from the perils of cats. Mainly crows, gulls and pigeons would enjoy the pieces of bread and then when the crumbs were left, the smaller birds like sparrows would appear to finish off all that was left. I'm also impressed by the grey squirrels, who live in the trees at the bottom of our garden; they venture out every day to find food and bury acorns in preparation for the winter months. These squirrels are often chased by our cats (and thankfully never caught) but although they're aware of the danger, they don't appear to be fazed by it; instead, they just get on with whatever they have to do.

It's long been known that gardens, with their greenery of foliage and colour of flowers and variety of aromas, can be very beneficial to one's mind and spirits and if you have a penchant for gardening, then so much the better because a certain fulfilment and satisfaction can be found too. I think that any hobby, pastime or occupation where you are totally absorbed in whatever you're doing, is food for the soul and makes you be *you*. It doesn't have to be trendy or impressive either.

I like to hear all the calls of wildlife and admire the beautiful countryside I'm afforded from my own home, away from the ongoing construction and development of more, apparently necessary, roads and houses. I want to sometimes feel the warm sun on my face as I ponder the next set of satisfying tasks for the day, week or month—as I do now, to an extent. But now the 'unmistakeable' sound of a woodpecker pummelling against a tree trunk, could also be the distant sound of a pneumatic drill either repairing old roads or preparing for new roads. Likewise, the high-pitched buzzing of a bumble bee, could equally be the sound of a circular saw from someone's building project. This is progress which will continue and probably increase as time goes by.

Thankfully, I can also immerse myself in some reading material, as and when I choose, and I can also find real pleasure and fulfilment in cooking—such as healthy and hearty breakfasts at the weekend. For any morning porridge, I will always use my happy wooden spoon (the wood grain coincidentally shows a happy face—see picture) and a friend pointed out that the same spoon has a sad face too, above the happy face—they were right, it does! It's still called my happy spoon though. So, until I can change my external environment, I can at least keep my internal soul happy and healthy and know that my pastimes will always be there for me—and there'll be more to come.

There's no need to rush anything either because there will always be things to do around the house, or things that need fixing or sorting out and so they'll all get done in good time and after I've spent my special pockets of time on my own agenda.

It's not to say that everyone would feel the same contentment from doing the same things of course but I think it's important to recognise your particular 'bliss factors' and allow the time for them—and alone if necessary, where you can bring all your faculties back together again, being mind, body, soul and spirit. Then you'll be ready for whatever life brings next and if it turns out to not be so good, then you'll be better equipped to deal with it before retreating back to your personal haven, where you can rethink and recharge all over again. This is what I find anyway and if, on the rare occasions, I feel so depleted and despondent about things (maybe from loss of sleep or whatever) then I'll start with a simple act like buying a magazine about houses, beauty or anything of interest and relax for a while with a hot drink. I know I'll feel better because there'll always be something to inspire me.

It was now November and a problem I thought had been resolved returned without warning: It was my mobile phone—suddenly not working at all one day, so it was obvious I'd be needing to replace it, and quickly (yet again). I had previously tried to keep the same design of phone I'd had for about twenty years, because it still held all my love messages from Tony and also the telephone numbers of people who have since passed away (I simply couldn't remove their memory) such as my mum and friend, Julie. So, with a big sigh, I mentioned to Tony that I might have to face up to the fact that I need to get a new modern phone after all.

"Hooray!" he shouted, "it's about time you climbed down off that sentimental horse of yours and threw that old phone in the bin where it belongs!"

Well, I didn't see this predicament in quite the same way and I wasn't going to put my old phone in the bin ever (but more likely, put it in the trunk with all my other keepsakes and phones which includes the early Motorola phone which resembles the shape of a house brick).

So, by the end of that day, I'd purchased my brand new phone with all the latest technology and all the other things I had no chance of getting my head around (having had to print off the user manual myself as it didn't actually come with any instructions!). Nevertheless, I was happy enough with my purchase and was able to keep my existing contract but with a smaller SIM card, so I retained my telephone number at least. Alas, my old messages and old contacts are now at peace with my old phone in the trunk of sentimentality.

On went my new and current contacts list and personalised screen picture and I must admit to feeling quite upbeat about this somewhat drastic and probably long-overdue change. I honestly didn't think I'd adapt so quickly but I did and furthermore, appreciated that this was a blessing in disguise because I would never need to use Tony's phone any more when we were out and about and I then needed to access information from the internet.

I think that the main reason why I'm not brilliantly clued up on computer technology is because throughout my working career (which included the very first introduction to PCs), I was only ever required to learn and use the computer software. If there was a problem with the computer itself, we would just call the 'IT' department and the system would be fixed in a thrice and so I didn't need to furnish my mind with such matters pertaining to IT troubleshooting.

I don't know whether large organisations still have the same kinds of IT departments but times have changed and I was recently reminded of this fact, once again: Tony and I were out walking one day and I noticed, on the ground, a long metal snake-like object and so I stopped and picked it up. It was a bracelet – unhitched from its clasp which probably explains why it fell from someone's wrist. It was a gold and silver colour in alternating blocks of links. Tony took it from my hand and stared closely at it.

"What are you doing?" I asked.

"Seeing if it's real gold and silver," he replied whilst still peering at it.

"It doesn't matter if it's valuable or not," I said, taking the bracelet back, "someone's lost it and it may be of sentimental value to them so I think we should hand it in to the police."

Tony agreed and so we went straight to the local police station where, to my surprise, we were told that they don't take lost property any more but *'well done for being honest and trying to hand it in'*.

I was stumped.

What if the person who'd lost the bracelet arrived at the police station to ask if it had been handed in? There was no mutual point of contact, such as that which used to exist in this way. I know that the police do a fantastic job these days in keeping law and order whilst under huge physical and financial pressure, so it is understandable that some things have to give. (I couldn't do their job because as soon as I see or hear about something bad, I automatically shut my eyes and put my hands over my ears whilst saying, "La, la, la, la, la" to make sure I don't hear anything. Yet I have no problem confronting anyone, calmly, if I have no choice). Thankfully, we are all different.

Now I was holding someone else's jewellery in

my hand. I had no intention of keeping it to myself so briefly considered the idea of putting an ad in the local paper with my phone number (the caller would then have to describe the bracelet) but this strategy seemed unlikely to reunite the bracelet with its owner. There was only one thing for it: to go back to the place where I'd found it, and put it back, in the vain hope that the real owner would come back and find it. The daytime was turning towards dusk and so with no-one else around but us, I went back and placed the bracelet back on the ground and said, "I hope your owner comes back."

The next day, I walked back to the same place and saw that the bracelet had gone. I don't need to think about it anymore.

This somewhat insignificant event was a classic case of identifying the difference between an inconvenience and a problem. The bracelet scenario was a slight inconvenience whereas my phone packing up was a problem. Both were now sorted but other matters played on my mind such as the houses for sale on our wish list and whether we should go and view them. This was more a case of reasons vs. excuses and I struggled to establish which was which.

Tony doesn't appear to give such matters as much thought and was very much of a mind that if we wanted to go and look at other properties, we should just take the time out to go. End of.

The particular factors which concerned me were:
- We've not yet sold our house (so not in a position to make any offers).

- Tony had a large workload commitment which ran right up to Christmas (he conceded).
- The car's engine warning light kept coming on randomly so needed sorting out ASAP.
- There'll be much more traffic on the road due to people out doing their Christmas shopping.
- News of a forthcoming snow storm 'sweeping Europe and the UK' was a slight concern.
- Some roads were still experiencing flooding due to heavy rain so driving conditions were poor.

In my mind it sounded like a list of excuses which I could have easily added to, and therefore talked myself out of going at all. But the thing was, two particular houses were worth viewing in my opinion and they could be sold by springtime. Opportunities do need to be seized, I know that, but I also know that serious decisions like buying houses, need to be planned carefully because only fools rush in—and get their hearts broken easily.

After a long deep breath, I thought about the time ahead which would be available to us when Tony's workload would have been completed, the car sorted, shoppers and traffic jams should be lighter and the weather would be the weather whatever week we'd chosen to drive in—indeed, it could be dry and very pleasant. The time we'd have available would be after Christmas as Tony had booked a few weeks off work then, so this could be a very fruitful time in many festive ways. The good thing was, we had the time to plan and decide. So, no problem.

In the meantime, I busied myself preparing for Christmas and made small improvements indoors to brighten the place up before the Christmas tree and all its paraphernalia came down from the loft. I'd cleaned and cleared the lounge as best I could and then rearranged and organised food storage cupboards in the kitchen. This was a potentially mundane task but practical and necessary. On the kitchen windowsill stood a tall slim glass of water with a bulb of garlic sitting on the top—the roots of which had been getting longer every day in conjunction with the green shoots above, growing taller. It wasn't my intention to grow garlic but this particular bulb was one of many from the supermarket and had started sprouting green shoots before I'd had a chance to cook with it and so I felt inclined to help it. Anyway, I now had a plan about the future of the bulb having researched useful information online. It was just as well that I had a plan as Tony asked me one day, "Do you mind telling me why you're growing garlic on the windowsill?"

"Oh yes, I must get some potting compost from the garden centre and I'll be potting it all up at the weekend, separating the cloves and putting them 4" apart in a large pot from the shed which I'll then put in that ½ barrel we've got, then it'll stay in the conservatory, getting watered until spring before I'll put outside, still in the pot and we may get some garlic bulbs from them in about nine months' time."

Tony looked understandably confused, then said,

"Why don't you save yourself the time and effort and put it in the bin now, then just buy some garlic when we next go shopping?!"

"I can't do that," I implored, "I've given it life now – I can't say, *'oh sorry, I've changed my mind now, so you'll have to go in the bin'*. No! I've committed to growing it so that's exactly what I will do. Either it grows or not."

And so, I have and have a healthy-looking crop growing perfectly well, as I write.

However, it's all very well skipping along through life in a little world of idealism, but often there's the likelihood of a sudden trip then splat! which brings reality back with a bang. This time it was news of a recall of washing machines due to a potentially faulty component that caused them to catch fire. My ears pricked up when I heard this news because ours was one such make of those to be recalled. Later that day, it was a relief to learn that our machine didn't fall within the manufacturing years in question and so it was safe to use. It occurred to me that, had we not recently got rid of our old washing machine (due to it filling up with water in the middle of the night on its own accord as I described) then we might have had a much worse experience so it had definitely been a blessing in disguise.

The car engine warning light seemed to be less of a blessing and would be needing proper attention from a garage despite Tony's efforts to sort the problem out by adding a cleaning fluid to the fuel tank as suggested by a local garage. Alas, it was now a case of needing to replace a particular valve which

Vanessa Bunting

would cost hundreds of pounds. Deep joy. I called the dealership where we'd originally purchased the car and explained our situation—of course there was a chance that I was wasting my time as it was 'outside' of the twelve-month warranty period now but I asked if they could help us or suggest anything to reduce the costs involved. The response was quite defensive and corporate in nature and so I reminded the dealer that I wasn't saying they were to blame – it's just one of those things (even though the car is supposed to be a 'quality assured' vehicle) - but I was giving them the chance to help us if they wanted to. They said they'd write to us in a few days after they'd discussed it.

Chances are we'd be footing the whole bill at a local garage, but if it needed fixing, then we had no choice. Ditto the boiler which was now on the blink and not getting up to full heat. So, a gas engineer checked it and suggested he put a cleaning fluid through the system (I'd heard that recently with the car!). But he would have to then return to drain the system fully—fine. The dreaded caveat being that if it didn't resolve the problem, we'd be needing a new part or a new boiler; either option costing hundreds of pounds (as with the car).

Some Christmas this was turning out to be and through it all, we had days and days of rain and more rain, as did most of the UK. The fields at the back of our garden were completely flooded and looked like an actual lake with ducks swimming on it too. As lovely as the scene was, I kept watch each day to ensure that the water didn't reach our garden. Over

146

the next week, the rain did stop and Tony and I both watched with interest as the water gradually receded each day to eventually become nothing more than a green open space once again.

Inevitably, our cats traipsed their muddy paws through the house and with the occasional mouse who, having been made homeless from the flooding, was now facing death. We saved a few mice and set them free out of the front door but felt so sorry for those who had perished. This is the downside of having cats as pets where there can be a constant clean-up due to water, mud, mice, etc. whilst the regular round of clean, feed, de-flea and so on continues.

This may have been the extent of our plight on this side of the fence, but the poor farmer on the other side of the fence must have been dealing with a much larger scale of flood water, mud, ruined crops, the welfare of livestock and probably financial concerns too. Many farmers were probably in the same situation but for those who lived and worked alone, life must be extremely difficult sometimes and so it's no wonder that depression can set in. This got me thinking: If there was a scheme in place where farmers could open their premises to the public as an interesting and unusual day out, every now and then, the farmers could showcase their farm's produce and receive some human contact and maybe an extra income too. I know there are health and safety concerns involved but I put the suggestion to Tony who agreed that this would be a worthwhile membership to have.

To my surprise, I found out that there is at least one scheme in place where participating farms *do* open their gates to the public at certain times of the year, and it's called 'Open Farm Sunday' (farmsunday.org). It's managed by LEAF (Linking Environment And Farming) and has numerous farmers throughout the UK who allow the public to enjoy their farm, farm shop, walks and activities for children, such as tractor rides. What a fabulous idea and the website has maps of farms concerned— which we would love to attend. Do take a look, if this interests you or your family in any way.

For now, throughout the UK this December, there remained flood warnings in place with many roads and towns still flooded. If Mother Nature had directed the rain towards the southern hemisphere instead, the masses of bush fires sweeping across Australia might have been more controllable and the catastrophic loss of flora and fauna may have been less severe. Some people actually lost their lives. It was such devastating news and another example of how unpredictable weather and global warming can affect all our lives to some extent.

I know that many readers will be aware of these events in the news but the reason why I am mentioning them here is because we are all linked by our lives and our homes – which are incredibly important because they provide us with sanctuary and security – unless they're threatened by the forces of nature or war. How can we ever feel completely at ease inside, if our immediate environment becomes precarious or even dangerous? I believe that, fundamentally, we have to feel safe and secure in wherever we call 'home' in order to fully function and flourish as human beings.

We might not be able to alter the weather right now, but we can look to building our homes away from the risks of flooding or fires and other natural disasters like earthquakes and volcanic eruptions. Unfortunately, there are too many people living with such threats every day who have no way of changing their circumstances—due to money mainly. The same predicament applies to those living within a war zone. In this respect, I feel guilty to be bleating on about my ideal home and its preferable location and environment. Shouldn't I just feel satisfied to have a roof over my head, food in my stomach and hot water to keep myself clean? Maybe I should but the reality is, I don't because the good fortune I felt in my younger years where I was blissfully happy in a home I loved, I want to experience again – with my loved ones – for however many days or years of my life I may have left to live.

Chapter 8

Up Drawbridge!

As another chapter, book and year closes, a new decade begins.

I would have liked, so much, to be relaying the details of a special home found at last with all the promise of becoming that, long awaited, Forever Home. It may be amongst the few houses still remaining on our online property list, to view but alas, it's not confirmed yet.

The plan to move house for the final time has been years in the making and maybe still months in securing but this is my dream and so I cannot accept that my life has already reached its fullest potential.

No one knows how long any dream will take to come to fruition but if you've done everything possible to make it happen, then surely you're justified in waiting for that door of opportunity to open. That said, I also know that the thoughts I had last year, last month or last week, may differ to the thoughts I have today because perceptions, priorities and desires can change over time. As new challenges and difficulties present themselves, we naturally evolve in our coping strategies and so have let go of the things which no longer serve us.

For the past decade I'd been working on finding someone to take my bottle stand idea forward, but this hasn't happened—it nearly did, but not quite. I have decided to let go of this particular quest and so will not be renewing the patent for the bottle stand. I have absolutely no regrets about the time, money or effort spent on supporting this project but I will certainly have regrets if I proceed with blind faith and false hopes which is all I have left. Therefore, this is one dream I am perfectly happy to give up, and in doing so, it will free my mind of bottle stands ever needing to materialise.

Another thought which had crossed my mind was the letting go of writing another book until I actually found that Forever Home and the holiday let business, which I can then write about as I *live the dream*. But isn't life all about those twists and turns in direction and the choices we make?

Would any true story be worth its salt if the basic foundations as to how it came about weren't told? My books would never have come about if I had carried on with my life as a single female working in the city, living life with friendship and contentment from her cosy cottage home. All my ideals were in place except for marriage and parenthood; as neither had interested me. This should have been my goal achieved after an insecure home-life as a child: being fraught with tension and angst, before moving to the flat in London with my mum until I took a company move to another county and lived in a flat for a few years until it was burgled. I then moved to a small Victorian house which I absolutely loved and lived in for ten years until new neighbours affected my wellbeing on a personal level and so I then moved to the cottage—which I expected to be my perfect and quiet idyll. Indeed, it was very quiet, inside the cottage and outside, but after a few weeks of moving in, I experienced an awakening within myself and an unexpected fountain of emotions ensued. I didn't even know they *existed* let alone existed in *me*.

Life had to change because I was completely overwhelmed by the intense goings-on deep within my soul. It was as if I had an inner child who was extremely unhappy. Never before had I made decisions based upon whether there were any emotional implications involved. I very much had the attitude that if anything needed doing or I needed to go anywhere, then I simply would. The move to the cottage was necessary and I dealt with the whole process as I had before but now the move had broken me, physically and mentally. I was worn out. On reflection it was no wonder why.

It did take time, patience, understanding and a certain amount of hard work to readjust to the person I am today; perhaps still scared in some respects, but I feel more complete as a human being and know how vulnerable we can all be, in a life that's fast-paced and sometimes very demanding.

I daresay that most people operate as a whole person most of the time, giving consideration to their personal needs when making decisions about their life but my books are about my life and experiences following a change of being. This is my way of documenting how involuntary changes needn't be detrimental to the greater scheme of things. Furthermore, to trust and use intuition when making decisions can bring a greater sense of resolve that the best decision was made by the whole self, together.

As I said, there are so many people living the very dream they followed from childhood and who are blissfully happy and truly fulfilled—which is ideal. These very rewards are there for everyone regardless of setbacks and circumstances. After all, a diamond sparkles and shines, even when shattered.

Anything can still happen on the house front and we are certainly in a better position to sell the house than before because Brexit should soon be completed. Our house has also had a few more improvements with redecoration and enhancements made.

I'm careful not to become dissatisfied with my current 'lot' because I still have every basic need I mentioned earlier, being...

- Fresh air
- Adequate sleep
- Warmth and security
- Cleanliness (home and self)
- Enough food to eat
- Enough water to drink
- Companionship and friendship – be it human, feline, flora or fauna
- Peace of mind - for most of the time

And now with the added bonus of a healthy

husband, healthy cats and a bumper crop of garlic growing in a half barrel!

Tony's list of ideals is also still in place...

- To be healthy
- Financially secure with a very nice house and car
- Happy and content with yours truly and the cats

To be focused on what we *do have,* is a positive step in itself because defining a dream doesn't necessarily make it happen. Neither do copious amounts of belief, enthusiasm, commitment and effort which Tony and I have expended thus far on the subject of moving house. So even with hard graft and time waited, you can *never* force the magic of chance to take effect.

As with past years, there were a few spooky moments in our house like the evening recently when we were watching TV. The lounge adjoins the conservatory and, as usual, the conservatory was lit by a lamp and the window blinds were closed. The adjoining sliding door was open so we could see into the conservatory. I was about to change channels on TV and was looking down at the remote control when suddenly Tony's head whipped around and looked towards the conservatory; as did our cat Whingey at the very same time. Tony put his hand to his chest and said he'd seen a shadow move past through the conservatory; clearly Whingey had seen it too but had stayed put, so wasn't frightened.

Nevertheless, I was glad to have been looking elsewhere at the time. I've had some spooky incidental moments during the day but not to the same extent or the washing machine scenario.

Now I am near the end of another book without the desired outcome. As much as I want to shape my world my way, and with my tribe, I remain accepting of life and the majority of gifts offered by living here. I feel that there is a reason why the house sale hasn't happened as yet and I know that there are some things in life – in fact many things in life – which are not ours to dictate or direct but we just need to keep faith and be there ready for when life and lifestyle does change, which it inevitably will. The only regret I have is that I'm not able to deliver more news in this respect but there were some magical twists of events recently, which I can relay before I close.

Just recently I heard an uplifting news clip about a young couple who'd planned to marry in a number of weeks to the find that the holiday company they'd booked their honeymoon with, had suddenly gone out of business. To make matters worse, just before their wedding day, the venue who were to be hosting the whole wedding ceremony, suddenly advised that they were to shut down due to debts! Nevertheless, the lovely couple still hoped to get married as planned and sought to make alternative arrangements elsewhere. They weren't deterred by the massive setbacks and didn't see their predicament as a sign to defer getting married at all. What resilience they showed, stars indeed. I wish them every success and future happiness.

For us in our nineteen years of marriage, we were looking to resolve the mundane issue regarding the temperamental central heating system and so decided to replace the boiler—not least because it's not fair to sell a house which has dodgy appliances. So, in one day we had a team of heating engineers busily traipsing around the house, soldering pipework amongst other engineering stuff and were clearly on track to finish by teatime. The cats were quite concerned by this invasion with Alice waiting outside on the patio in the cold and damp for most of the day, and her sister Clipsey retreating to her newfound hiding place—in the desk pedestal cabinet which she'd accessed by squeezing her way through, behind the desk. I'd opened the cabinet door at lunchtime and fed her some cat treats. Sure enough, by late afternoon, the new boiler was installed and running well with all the radiators around the house scorching hot again. By bedtime, all the cats were suitably warm indoors and sleeping soundly their usual places. This pleased me more than having the heating fixed and I was once again reminded of the dreadful upheaval which would ensue in the event of a complete house move.

With regard to the car, there was a week of highs and lows after we'd decided to trade it in for another car we'd found at another dealership. It was all very rushed but Tony needed a reliable car for work and so we found a slightly larger but younger car at a garage in another town. It had fitted all the criteria we were looking for and so we paid a deposit and were due to complete the deal the following week.

Would you believe that the day before we were to collect the new car, an engine warning light came on in *our* car! Isn't it typical? It was too late to do anything but carry on with the deal but tell the garage about the warning light. Doing that would mean we would have to accept that the deal may be off, and we'd need to get the car repaired again and keep it, as we really wouldn't be able to afford to buy anything else.

The night before we were due to go to the garage, Tony looked extremely stressed with eyes full of burden and dark shadows below them. I tried to comfort him and reassure him that whatever happened, we'd have a reliable car in the end. It was entirely down to the discretion of the car dealer.

The next morning, we were relaying the 'problem' to the car salesman who then went and had a long chat with his manager before returning to say that we'd have to go and get the car repaired and then return in order to complete the deal.

"No," Tony and I said having already discussed that suggestion "that's not an option for us because if we had to spend more on our car, we'll need our deposit back to pay for it and so the deal will be off, with regret."

The salesman scurried off again to seek further advice and was probably enjoying his day just about as much as we were at that point. A deal is a deal until any factors change; and ours had. It was no-one's fault but just one of those things. A while later, the salesman returned with his boss who said quite calmly that they would need to put our car in their workshop to see exactly what the problem was. We would all then know what was going on. It would take a few hours so could we leave it with them and they could lend us a car to go home if we wanted? We thanked them for their generous offer, but it wasn't necessary as we would find a coffee shop somewhere and return in a few hours.

On this amicable note, we walked off, hand in hand, to head for the nearest venue for some much-needed caffeine! I'm sure the garage would have provided coffee and let us wait somewhere but we all needed our space and time to think. The situation wasn't looking good but what can you do but be honest and open. By a strange coincidence, this had happened to us once before when we'd traded our car in and on the very day, at the new garage, the engine warning light came on! At that time, the people weren't bothered and said their workshop would fix whatever was wrong. This was a different time, a different dealership and a very different deal.

After our coffee, we strolled along a few streets past bustling roads, flats and businesses towards a little antique shop we'd visited before. For me it was the perfect venue in which to kill time and browse the many artefacts of yesteryear, reminiscing about our aunts and uncles having this type of tea-set or that type of glass fish. The relaxing atmosphere was a perfect tonic for both of us I'm sure and amidst a sea of ceramics at one side of the shop, I spotted a small vase, painted in muted colours of cream, russet, pale green and beige. Not a particular design as such but quite individual, with a matt finish. It would look lovely on our mantelpiece and Tony agreed. I held on to the vase as there was another couple in the shop although they seemed more concerned with the maker's mark underneath each item, so weren't a threat to me and my humble taste.

Then I saw a small picture on the wall, amongst many others. A watercolour, maybe a print, behind a rustic wooden and glass frame, depicting a countryside scene of fields and crops being harvested. The horses, carts and people suggested a time dating back to a few hundred years perhaps and the hills and mountains in the background, very much reminded me of Wales, although it could have been anywhere in Europe or the world for that matter. The picture of my dream destination was in my other hand now and so I went to the till to pay. I mentioned to the lady shopkeeper how lovely it was to be drawn to certain pieces and the pleasure they give, so 'thank you'. She smiled at me and then looked over my shoulder at the couple deep in discussion about a ceramic plate they'd turned over. She looked back at me and said, "You are very welcome to visit my shop, any time."

I knew what she meant.

Tony and I left the shop and made our way back to the garage. We were to learn of our fate with the car. It occurred to me that I had thought of our car as being 'it' for the next few years, but it had turned out not to be the case and had cost us dearly. What if this happened when we move and think that our home is our Forever Home and it too becomes a money pit?! Quick! Time to think positive thoughts like my latest buys for the home and the difference they'll make! Phew, that's better.

Back at the garage, we received the brilliant news that the deal was on and our car was okay—it just needed some re-jigging of the computer and the message removed. We were so relieved. Tony asked how much a towbar would cost to be fitted to the new car but after hearing the price of £900, said we'd leave it for now! (I'm not sure when we'd be having a spare £900 but without the towbar, the trailer is completely useless.)

So, after all the necessary paperwork was completed, we left the garage in our new (and hopefully 'improved') car. The seats were very comfortable, so better for Tony's back and the drive felt very smooth and quiet. It was just the job and we were both impressed and pleased with our choice.

Back home, I put that lovely pot on the mantelpiece and what an instant artistic upgrade it made, so another good choice. I put the kettle on for tea and then walked around the house with the picture to see where was best and not too bright in terms of sunlight in case it faded. The stairs would be best, and I would then see it and be reminded of my dream every day. Just then Tony came in. He'd been outside looking over the car in more detail. He smiled and said, "Do you want the good news or the brilliant news?"

"Go on then," I answered.

"Well, we don't need to buy a towbar, and the reason is, it has one already! A detachable tow bar; I found it in a bag at the back of the boot. I thought it was the jack at first but it's a tow bar and the electrics are under the car and ready to go!"

He was so thrilled. Isn't it lovely to find something unexpectedly—almost a gift, and so timely too?

We had a cup of tea and enthused about our 'finds' that day and how we no longer need to worry about the car. It was lovely to see Tony smiling again; then off he went outside to the car whilst I fixed up the little picture on the stairs. I placed it at eye-level on the halfway landing so it could be seen close up. I marvelled at the soft colours of blue, creams, green and russet (much like the colours of the little pot I'd purchased at the same time). There was no artist's name I could see but the honesty of the picture and subject matter, meant so much to me personally. I was now able to look closely at the picture and its scenery with those craggy hills in the distance. Then I saw to the left of the picture, a hill topped with a structure of some kind. I looked closer – yes it was a castle – an ivory coloured castle. Well, what are the chances of having a castle in the background of a landscape picture? This was another special find of the day and would now serve like a bulwark itself, by defending my hopes and dreams. Our day had started with trepidation and angst but had ended with surprise and reassurance for both of us.

Never give up on *your* dreams, even if they change or morph into something else. Strange and special things happen—and they can happen when you least expect them to.

Until next time, dear reader.

From the Author of:

Forever Home Within
Forever Home Within ~ and Beyond!
Forever Home Within ~ Here And Now
Forever Home Within ~ Silently Strong

More accounts of everyday life and thoughts in this
true story about fulfilling a dream
and living that dream in a Forever Home which must
be out there somewhere – shouldn't it?

Living in Essex, England with her husband and 5
cats, Vanessa's professional career spanned three
decades. She has written various articles for
magazines and newsletters.

For more information, please visit the website:
www.foreverhomewithin.com

BV - #0001 - 070520 - C2 - 203/127/9 - PB - 9781912505821